e Russian Lieutenant's Woman

The Russian Lieutenant's Woman

A TRUE STORY OF PASSION, LOVE AND BETRAYAL

BARBARA DAVIES

HODDER

British Library Cataloguing in Publication Data
A record for this book is available from the British Library

ISBN 978 0340 91050 4

Typeset in Granjon by Avon DataSet Ltd,
Bidford on Avon, Warwickshire

Printed and bound in Great Britain by
Clays Ltd, St Ives plc

The paper and board used in this paperback are natural
recyclable products made from wood grown in sustainable forests.
The manufacturing processes conform to the environmental
regulations of the country of origin.

Hodder & Stoughton
A Division of Hodder Headline Ltd
338 Euston Road
London NW1 3BH
www.madaboutbooks.com

For A.N. J. D. D.

Prologue

I didn't see your father walk into the room.

It was as if he suddenly appeared across the desk from me, immaculate in his dark green military uniform. The first time I saw him he was sideways on, motionless. I stared at his strong nose and cheekbone and wondered how long he'd been sitting there before I had noticed him.

I opened my mouth without thinking: 'Look, Olga. He's beautiful.'

The only person in the room who understood what I had said looked up from the report she had been translating from Russian into English and followed my gaze.

'Yes,' said Olga matter-of-factly. 'I think you may be right.'

Lieutenant Dmitry Andreyevich Valinsky swivelled in his chair towards me, took off his hat and smiled.

When I look at you now, I think of that smile as the moment that we started creating you.

* * *

It is late now. I am writing this at the kitchen table in our little flat.

You are fast asleep in your bed. You have kicked off the covers and your small pink hand is clutching your toy puppy.

In a moment, I will walk into the bedroom so I can watch you sleep.

I will smooth my hand across your soft cheeks and bed-tangled golden hair. I will brush my lips against your temple and hush you when you stir.

Anyinky, malinky, horoshinky. Sleep little Anya, little beauty, little angel.

If I pause from tapping on the keyboard in front of me and sit absolutely still, I can just hear your gentle breaths whispering across the hall.

I heard you a moment ago – just a half-cry as you turned in your sleep, your pearly eyelids fluttering in childish thought.

Are you dreaming my darling? Is your tiny head already filled with thoughts and pictures snatched from the day? Do you know yet how remarkable your life is? In the morning, you will open your eyes again. They are clear and blue and questioning.

Be patient, my love.

When you are older, I will tell you a story about a small town far away in the Ural mountains, and the beautiful blue-eyed lieutenant who is your father.

It will be your story – even when I am no longer here to tell it.

1

In an office, somewhere in the depths of the Bely Lebed Prison Colony in the Urals, Olga was poring over the pages of the report with her finger, deciphering the Russian Cyrillic script as she went. She skimmed over the mundane parts and read the juiciest out loud with relish.

'Oh, this bit is great! It says here that he liked to remove their eyes with a stick and eat parts of their breasts!'

I wrote quickly in shorthand, stopping now and then to check the spelling of the unfamiliar-sounding names of the murderer and his thirty or so victims, and to stare at the beautiful lieutenant sitting opposite me.

My pen hovered above the page. He was as still as a statue. His blue eyes crinkled at the edges and his smooth, dark lips tightened mischievously into dimples curving up towards sharp cheekbones. His thick, cropped hair was so dark it was almost black.

'Vladimir Bratilov,' said Olga, jolting me out of thought. 'B-r-a-t-i-l-o-v.'

'Look Olga, he's beautiful . . .'

It wasn't my idea to interview a cannibal serial killer.

'I want to know what it feels like to sit in a room with one,' enthused the *Daily Mirror*'s features editor. 'He's bound to have something interesting to say. And get some pictures of the two of you together.'

As a tabloid journalist, it was the most bizarre request I had ever received. Even so, I gave him the standard sunny response I always mustered when faced with a 'mission impossible'.

'Fine. No problem. Leave it with me.'

I carefully copied down everything Olga told me into a spiral-bound reporter's notebook: during a three-year reign of terror, Bratilov stalked the streets of Lysva, evading capture by the town's militia. Olga Kosenko, raped and strangled; Maria Shetsova, a seventeen-year-old he offered to walk home from a nightclub, found murdered and mutilated in Lysva's Pushkin Park; Alvira Kanzeparova, her eyes gouged out; Valentina Morozova, a pretty blonde fourteen-year-old who went out to buy bread for her brother's birthday party. Her father found her an hour later, naked and strangled, behind a tree near her home; Anna Marakulina – Bratilov attacked her from behind before realising he knew her.

Olga read from an interview with a prison psychologist. Bratilov recalled how he tried to pretend it was all a big joke. He jostled Anna and laughed and offered her a cigarette. While they smoked, he could see in her face that she didn't believe him. She was nervous. She was trying to stay calm, but he could sense the hysteria welling up inside her. When he realised he had failed to fool her, he raped her and beat her to death.

In the corner of the room, Major Boris Kapolev, the officer responsible for Bratilov at the prison, was watching us closely. He sat on his desk and dragged heavily on a cigarette. He was excluded from our excited whispers, just as I was excluded from his conversation with Olga.

'He wants to know if you are from London,' she said, looking up from the file when he asked her the question.

'Da,' I said, smiling at him and nodding.

I continued writing.

Son of wealthy factory manager.
Privileged upbringing but failure at school.
Humiliating sexual encounter aged 14 with older woman.

Boris ground out his cigarette in a glass ashtray and spoke again. His pale grey, wolf eyes darted back and forth between us.

'He asks how long you've been a journalist,' said Olga, this time without looking up from the page she was studying.

National Service then job as railway worker.
Killed first victim when he was 21.

'Have you ever felt cold like this?' asked Boris. Olga translated the question and my reply – an exaggerated, dramatic 'no', suitably deferential to a winter more cruel than anything England could ever inflict.

We carried on. In the margin of one typed psychiatric report, a doctor had noted something Bratilov had told him during one of their meetings.

'When I see a woman, I just want to attack her straight-away.'

The doctor wrote: 'He has never shown any remorse for his crimes. He has no feeling. No morality.'

Eventually, Olga turned the final page of the report and I laid down my pen. Outside, the frozen Urals sky was already turning blue-black. Snowflakes tumbled through the artificial yellow light cast out of the prison office window.

Beneath his mouse-coloured hair, Boris's skin was waxy and pale. He explained the rules of engagement for the interview the following day and outlined the arrangements for the *Mirror*'s photographer, Chris, who had still not arrived from Moscow. He looked straight at me when he spoke, not at Olga, translating at his side.

'You mustn't go within an arm's reach of him at any time. Watch your hair and keep your face and hands back. Be careful he can't reach you under the table with his legs. He has been warned if he moves, the meeting will be terminated.'

I nodded. I was smiling. My skin was prickling with excite-ment. I was thinking how wonderful his dramatic words would look in my finished newspaper article.

2

The first time I saw my name in print was as a twenty-three-year-old trainee reporter at the *Croydon Advertiser*. It was June 1995. I had been told to write an article about an enormous crater appearing in a leafy residential street, which had recently undergone major repairs. I put in a terrible pun about long-suffering residents facing a 'hole new problem', which somehow got past the subeditors and on to the page. When the newspaper came out that Friday, I set aside four copies and carefully cut out my article from each. I placed them in envelopes and posted them off to my mother and stepfather, father and stepmother, my brother and my grandmother.

The accompanying note proclaimed my arrival: 'My first byline!'

One Thursday afternoon about a month later, I was alone in the newsroom with the editor. The paper had just gone to press for the week and the staff had retired to the Royal Oak across the road, when the call came that an armed raid was taking place at a railway mail depot a few miles away in Selhurst.

I caught a bus and arrived in time to see the pool of blood left when police had shot one of the raiders, and there was also an elegant, leggy reporter from the *Sun* climbing out of a red sports car, talking animatedly on her mobile phone. I made a reverse-charge call to the office on a pub payphone and the editor took down my shaky, clumsy report. The following day I had the front-page splash and when, after work, I carried it home to my tiny, airless attic bedsit, I smoothed the silky broadsheet across the stained brown and gold carpet and quivered with pride.

Five years on, I was still addicted to the adrenaline rush but played for higher stakes.

After two years, I said goodbye to my colleagues at the *Advertiser* offices on the A23 near Purley in Surrey, and set about conquering national newspapers with a hunger so intense it was like madness.

I knocked on the doors of bereaved parents and spied on unfaithful actors, pop stars, sport stars and their lovers. I flew above the Adriatic in the cockpit of an RAF refuelling plane and spent a day in a huge sports hall, queuing up with thousands of people waiting to be hugged by a visiting white-robed Indian mystic.

I chased two escaped Tamworth pigs around a field in Wiltshire, and travelled across Iraq with a former RAF navigator in an enormous black GMC truck brought over the border from Kuwait.

During three years as a national newspaper journalist, I played chess against World Chess Grandmaster Garry Kasparov, and witnessed the closure of Chernobyl in the Ukraine. I once spent New Year's Day in Trafalgar Square with a homeless heroin addict, then drove to a run-down housing estate in Portsmouth to watch screeching vigilante mothers attempting to lynch a suspected paedophile living among them.

There was a baby-snatch in Essex, a Bournemouth scout mistress who 'waggled the toggle' of one of her underage charges, the bloodshed of the Omagh bombing, a murdered WPC in East London, an avalanche in the Austrian Alps. Hours after Michael Hutchence hanged himself in a Sydney hotel room, I stood with a pack of reporters and photographers in the middle of the road outside Paula Yates' Chelsea home listening to her hysterical screams of grief through the open windows.

Once, in the line of duty, I even allowed my precious long red locks to be snipped off in the Mayfair salon of the Prime Minister's hairdresser, in a bid to pick up some gossip about him. It was the only time I was ever reported to the Press Complaints Commission for extracting information by deception.

When the phone rang, nothing was too much when it came to furthering my career. I earned a reputation among friends and family for being unreliable and unavailable. I would accept invitations to parties or weekends away and then cancel at the last minute. I always ruined family Christmases. But no one ever suggested there might be a more sensible way to earn a living.

'How exciting, darling!' my mother would say when I telephoned to cancel yet another visit. 'Don't worry at all. Call us when you get back.'

Weekly food shops became pointless. A trip to the supermarket on a Saturday guaranteed I would be sent away the following day. On one occasion, during a series of Allied airstrikes on targets in Serbia and Kosovo, I was sent to RAF Bruggen near Mönchengladbach in Germany on 'widow watch'. I returned home a month later to do battle with a biological disaster waiting inside my fridge.

I kept my passport with me at all times and an overnight bag in the boot of my car, packed with a selection of clothes for warm and cool climates.

I only ever forgot it once. I had arrived home at two in the morning from Belgium, where I had been trotting around the greens in pursuit of 'love rat' golfer Nick Faldo. I carried the small black bag into my flat, planning to empty and repack it. When I set off for the office the next morning, tiredness made me forget it. Five hours later, I was on a plane to Malaga with only the clothes I was wearing. I stepped through the heat-haze on to the Spanish tarmac wearing a black cashmere coat over a woollen suit.

When I wasn't abroad, my car became a second home. During days spent parked outside people's houses, the front passenger footwell would gradually fill up with empty petrol station sandwich wrappers, squashed cigarette cartons, scrunched-up road maps and old newspapers. The door pockets were filled with rotten brown apple cores and greasy crisp packets. The ashtray bulged with acrid-smelling butts. A fine layer of dust and ash coated the dashboard and seats.

Mostly I tried to ignore it. I lost count of the number of times I pulled up in the parking space outside my flat late at night and thought: 'I'll clean it up tomorrow.' I began to feel as if I was drowning.

My life was a mess. Inevitably, so was my love life.

* * *

I learned early on that love was a tricky business. One of my earliest memories, aged four, was seeing my mother's enormous chest freezer strapped on to a trailer on the drive outside our little semi-detached house near Southampton. I wondered why it wasn't in the garage, making its lovely pulsing, whirring noise. There was a commotion on the drive, some of the neighbours came out into their front gardens to have a look, and then I watched as the trailer and the freezer roared off down the road and disappeared around the corner. I couldn't see who was driving, but I understood that the freezer had gone for ever and taken my mother with it.

She had found true love, and I soon understood that such a love could bind you up or shut you out.

My father put his arms around my older brother and me. 'Only we three matter now,' he said.

My mother, when we visited her every fortnight, said very little except that she loved us both.

She was an enigma. But during visits to the house where she lived with my stepfather, I saw tantalising glimpses of her.

There were photographs of her in long, flowing Indian-print dresses and straw hats, sitting in long grass on the banks of a river somewhere in France, painting and sipping red *vin de pays*. She looked happy and beautiful.

In the bedroom where I slept at her newly built home, there was a box of old clothes in a cupboard. Inside the box was a black, silky, lacy nightdress. It was the most sensuous thing I had ever seen. I thought it was the sort of thing a princess might wear, but darker, more mysterious. I rubbed it against my cheek. In the middle of the night, when she and my stepfather were asleep, I used to put it on and then creep to the bathroom and look for her make-up. I darkened my lashes with her mascara and made my lips conker red and then stood tiptoe on the toilet seat, holding on to the towel rail and leaning out precariously so I could see myself in the mirror. I stared at my reflection. I wanted to be like her.

On Sunday evenings, when our fortnightly visits were drawing to an end and it was time for my stepfather to drive me and my brother home, she would have already changed into one of her ankle-length kaftans and started clearing the toys away out of sight. We pulled out of the drive to the fading sound of a Mozart horn concerto. Candles flickered seductively at the windows.

In the car on the way home, I dug my fingertips into my legs to stop myself crying.

'It hurts me to see you cry,' my father once said. I didn't want to hurt him. I became a skilled dissembler.

Usually I held my breath until I could get to my bedroom and crawl in among the soft toys and boxes of games at the bottom of the built-in wardrobe. Or I waited for the Sunday evening bath I shared with my brother.

Under the cover of steam and water, I let the silent tears flow freely and wiped them away with the flannel my anxious brother handed me when we heard my father's footsteps on the stairs.

He's coming! Stop now! Quickly! He's coming!

One Sunday evening when I was about seven years old, I didn't cry at all. My father said we were going to take our little blue boat out on one of our trips down the River Hamble.

It was our favourite treat, and I didn't feel sad any more. We were going to tie our boat up to the wooden pontoon at the edge of The Jolly Sailor pub. We would have Coca-Cola in cold dewy bottles, and we'd blow bubbles with our striped straws until the sticky brown liquid erupted through the bottle neck and spilt all over our hands. While my father went inside and drank beer from a glass mug with a handle, my brother and I liked to lie on our bellies on the pontoon and press our faces against the smooth planks of wood, staring between the gaps at the mossy green water moving beneath us.

The boat slowed down as we approached the jetty in front of the pub. The sun was already setting. Outside, the tables were covered in glasses and empty packets of crisps. The light hum of conversation came whispering across the water. Barefooted children played at the river's edge and looked enviously at my brother and I perched on the front of our boat in our life jackets.

Then I saw my mother sitting at one of the tables with her husband. She looked like a film star. She had changed her clothes since I'd said goodbye to her a few hours earlier. Her shoulder-length dark hair was held up on top of her head by tortoiseshell combs. She was wearing a long flowery dress. She and my stepfather looked up and saw us in our little boat. They whispered to each other quickly and she smiled at us gracefully, giving nothing away.

Our two worlds were about to collide. My father's face was contorted with awkwardness. For a moment he seemed paralysed. Then, his hands manipulated the controls and the boat accelerated away from the jetty. He said: 'Never mind, we'll go somewhere else.' My mother didn't watch us go. But I watched her. Her bare tanned shoulders had turned back towards her husband. She got smaller and smaller until we slipped round the curve of the river and I couldn't see her any more.

When I was old enough to think about such things, I comforted myself with the thought that my future husband was out there somewhere, as unaware of me as I was of him. One day, I was sure, he would find me and we would drink wine and play Mozart in the candlelight.

My time would come, but I would have to be patient.

My first love, Richard, found me at a sixth-form party held at The Albert Tavern nightclub on South Parade pier in Southsea. It was 4 July 1989. I was a seventeen-year-old A-level student, wrapped up in my own little romantic world of Keats' poems and Thomas Hardy novels. I was mad about The Cult, Rachmaninov and All About Eve. I wore vintage Laura Ashley and Dr Marten boots, scented my hair with rosemary oil and dreamed of romance and an idyllic, mythical, pre-Raphaelite past. Above the dirge of music on the night we met, Richard held my hands in his and I watched in amazement as his brown eyes danced with enchantment at my noisy chatter. I didn't know that I could make a man feel like that. When he gently drew my wrists towards him, I was already in love.

It was the summer holiday. Five days after the night we met, I took my bicycle across Portsmouth harbour on the Gosport ferry and met Richard at the other side. I wondered if daylight would break the enchantment spell of a week before.

He was wearing ripped jeans, cowboy boots and an old-fashioned collarless white shirt from a vintage clothing shop in

Southsea. The scent of his warm skin, flushed from the exertion of cycling, rose through the crisp white cotton and made me tremble.

We rode along the beach road from Gosport towards Lee-on-Solent; along Marine Parade with its cafes and ice-cream parlours and shop exteriors crowded with children's inflatable speedboats and dolphins. The beach was full with children paddling and building sandcastles, pensioners swimming, picnics spread out. The warm sea breeze mingled with the sounds of their voices. We whizzed past them, turning our heads out towards the sea.

Richard powered ahead of me, standing on his pedals to work up speed. I struggled to keep up with him. Occasionally, he stopped completely to let me catch up and I could hear the sound of his voice carried on the wind:

Come on!

My heart was pounding tightly against my rib cage, I could hardly breathe but I kept pedalling hard. The beachside shops were replaced by pebble-dashed seafront houses, then HMS *Daedalus* where a red and white coastguard helicopter sat next to a giant hovercraft. Richard's bike turned sharply to the left. I followed him into Salterns Road, and silence enveloped us. Hedgerows blotted out the wind. I could hear my bicycle wheels clicking and whirring as they turned. My lips tasted salty. Richard was alongside me now, looking across and smiling. We were too out of breath to talk. A shock of golden brown hair had fallen across his tanned face. At the end of the road, we turned left once more into Hill Head, past the Osborne View pub which looked across the Solent to Queen Victoria's home on the Isle of Wight on one side and the giant chimney of Fawley power station on the other.

We left our bikes on their sides on the driveway of his parents' home, and drank pint-glassfuls of icy Perrier water in the kitchen. Upstairs in his room, we kissed for the first time since the night we had met. My skin was as flushed as his now. Our bodies smelt sweet.

Later we opened his bedroom window and placed the stereo on the table beside it. Mozart's Piano Concerto No. 21 in C Major trickled gently across the hot summer garden. I sat on the swing and Richard pushed me while the music played. I could feel the warm pressure of his hands against my back every time I swung back towards him. When the swing reached the uppermost point of its arc, I could see right to the end of the garden and over the bird sanctuary and the setting sun beyond it. I was flying with the piano notes floating through the still evening air. Eventually, the swing slowed down. Richard's hands moved down to my waist. He drew the swing to a standstill and buried his lips in my neck.

A year later, we were still together. We were still playing Mozart. We lit candles in his bedroom and drank bottles of blood red St Emilion wine. He was mine and I was his, and I thought I knew everything there was to know about love.

But I had a premonition about what would happen to us.

Once, after spending the weekend with him at his parents' house, I drove away in my father's white VW Golf Diesel. I had promised to be back home by Sunday afternoon, but I panicked and turned the car around and drove back to Richard's house. I roared into the steep drive, pulled on the handbrake, jumped out and ran through the open front door. His mother was in the kitchen peeling potatoes.

'Where is he?' I said desperately.

'Upstairs,' she said, nodding her head upwards towards the ceiling.

Richard was in the bathroom. He had just been for a run along the beach and was about to take a shower.

I buried my face against his chest and cried until there were dark wet patches across his navy blue t-shirt. He held me and stroked my hair but he didn't understand.

The future loomed ahead of me like a deep, dark canyon, calling me on and away from him. I could see what lay ahead and it made me weary.

I saw all the things I would have to achieve in life and I knew that the struggle would be unending. I would go to university, sit my finals, get my degree, battle my way into my chosen career. I was meant to want all these things, but I didn't want to go on.

To have ignored untasted experiences would have been to spurn the very purpose of life and, aged seventeen, I was certain that that was a terrible crime.

Clutched to his chest in the bathroom, I sobbed for the time when I would no longer be his. The thought of what lay ahead made me feel tired. I wanted to make everything stop, and stay with him for ever. It was like the Keats poem we were studying at school – except that on my Grecian urn, Richard and I stood among the men and gods and maidens. Captured in time. Together for ever.

'More happy love! More happy, happy love!
For ever warm and still to be enjoy'd . . .'

But it wasn't for ever. My fears about the future proved to be justified.

Richard left home to start officer training at the Royal Naval College in Dartmouth. I was offered a place to study history at Oxford. A year later, we had parted.

At Oxford I met Simon, a cerebral, intense German and philosophy student from Belfast, who was so besotted with me that I kept trying to find ways of testing his love. Once I woke him up at 6 a.m., sighed, and told him I was dying for a cigarette. Outside it was pouring with rain. He jumped out of bed, threw on some clothes and happily trotted out into the dark February morning to find a newsagent. He returned with a packet of Marlboro. He lit one and passed it to me as I lay warm beneath the blankets of his narrow college bed. I knew it would never work.

I replaced him with Shaun, whose father had been a pop star in the seventies. He was crazy and funny and unpredictable. He made me laugh more than any man I had ever met. He also made me cry with alarming frequency. His own mother warned me about him when I went to stay at their house in Hertfordshire. She sat me down with a cigarette and a cup of coffee and said that a lot of girls rang the house. There was pity on her face.

Then there was Iain – a jealous, controlling trainee barrister whose fondness for reading poetry out loud to me became rather annoying – and Rudi Rinaldi, an engineering student from Florence. We met in a cafe near the church of Santa Croce while

I was studying Italian during the long summer holiday. I floated in on a wave of long skirts and petticoats, imagining myself to be Lucy from Forster's *A Room With A View*, and he asked me to sit at his table.

We kissed at sunset overlooking the city in Piazzale Michelangiolo, and he asked me to stay with him for ever.

I pictured myself barefoot, pregnant, padding around a big kitchen, cooking spaghetti for him.

'You will go back to England and forget me,' he said sadly. I shook my head and protested: 'No, Rudi! No!'

Then one evening he took me out for dinner and shouted at me while flinging his jacket around my bare, freckled shoulders. I decided it would be better to go back to Oxford and finish my degree.

In my twenties, things went from bad to worse.

There were men who loved me more than I loved them, and men I loved who didn't love me. There were commitmentphobes and liars and men so desperate to settle down that I knew their love had little to do with me. Sometimes I focused on work and didn't bother with men, and sometimes I yearned for a soul mate. Sometimes there was Mr B, my married lover, and sometimes, when I felt strong and independent and self-contained, there wasn't.

Somewhere along the line, I had turned into one of those women who didn't get married.

By the time I was twenty-eight, I was starting to get a bad feeling about it.

My older married brother summed it up for me rather harshly: 'Your lifestyle hardly makes you an attractive proposition,' he said.

I told him I didn't think that was very romantic, and he laughed in despair.

Two months before I went to Russia, I tried to bring some order to the chaos of my life. I bought my first flat.

Mr B helped me move from the rented room in Balham where we had become lovers two years before to a small one-bedroom flat in Westminster, bought with a tiny deposit and a huge mortgage. We argued in the morning. He had promised to come early to help me but then let me down – with no apology. He simply didn't turn up. When I called to find out where he was, he casually mentioned that he had a few errands to run and would arrive later. It was the same old story. In a relationship founded on lies, you are always lied to. Lied to and let down.

When he finally turned up on removal day, I sulked – which always irritated him. Once the removal men had brought the last box up the three flights of stairs to the new flat and been paid, they left and I closed my front door behind them.

Mr B presented me with a warm bottle of champagne.

'So you can celebrate later,' he said sheepishly.

He didn't need to add that he wouldn't be there to share it with me.

That first night in my new home, the champagne helped numb the hollowness as I started unpacking alone.

Eventually, when the bottle was three-quarters empty, I stopped putting things away. I pumped up the inflatable mattress I had bought to sleep on until I could afford to buy a bed, and unpacked my duvet.

I pictured Mr B lying asleep next to his wife in their house somewhere in north London. I always liked to imagine them back to back, with at least a foot between them. Him in pyjamas. Her in a thick woolly nightdress. I tried not to think about their two young children sleeping in the other bedrooms.

We met at Ascot on 17 June 1999. It was Ladies' Day and my twenty-seventh birthday. He was funny and attentive and flirtatious. It would have been too obvious to ask if he was single.

I tried to be cunning. The conversation had steered round to the subject of children.

'How many do you have?' I asked, hoping he would look shocked and reply, 'None!'

When he rolled his eyes and said, 'Two,' my heart sank. I smiled through a wave of disappointment.

He asked me to meet him later for a drink to celebrate my birthday. I said yes, but I knew I wouldn't turn up. He belonged to somebody else.

I drove home that evening and thought that was the end of it. But a few weeks later, I bumped into him again in a bar. He gave me a hurt, accusing look that baffled me.

Another two weeks later, he had managed to get my telephone number. He called me.

'I lost my camera,' he said feebly. 'I wondered if you noticed it in the bar at all.'

I told him I hadn't.

'Never mind,' he said. He asked me to meet him for lunch. Then dinner. We became lovers.

Any thoughts that I was doing something wrong were quickly brushed away.

When my blissfully happy mother had met the man who

would become her second husband, they were both married to other people. As a child, well-meaning adults told me all the time: 'They loved each other. You can't blame them for what they did.'

My grief was justified by their extraordinary love for each other. I had to forgive.

Days and weeks passed by. I sank deeper and deeper. When I realised I was falling in love with Mr B, I cried and tried to end it.

'I don't want to live half a life,' I told him.

He promised me it wouldn't be like that. He said he wanted to look after me.

Once, I was having problems sleeping. My neck felt sore. The day after I had moaned about it to Mr B there was a knock at the front door. I opened it to find a taxi driver standing there with two enormous bright yellow Selfridges carrier bags. Behind him, the loud diesel engine of his black cab was still running.

Inside the bags were four enormous goosedown pillows and smooth white Egyptian cotton cases.

I made up the bed. The room was brilliant white. It dazzled me.

I thought that if I walked away from him, then I might also be walking away from the rare, precious kind of love my mother had found.

People made mistakes. It wasn't right that someone should be punished for making the wrong choice.

My love for him grew and grew until I didn't need to justify it to myself any more.

*

I climbed on to the inflatable mattress. My head was spinning when I lay it on the crumpled pillow.

I knew that it was finally over; that Mr B would never leave; that with him I would always be alone.

I pictured myself in years to come, withered, empty, childless.

I wondered how I had managed to get it all so wrong.

The shrill ring of my mobile phone cut into my sleep. My head ached from the champagne, and it took me a couple of seconds to remember where I was. I rolled off the inflatable mattress and grabbed my phone.

It was my boss – 'begging' me for a favour.

'I know you've just moved into your new flat,' he cooed, 'but you're the only person I can trust.' Meaning, of course, that everyone else he had asked had something planned for that Saturday afternoon.

The interview, just hours away, was with a well-known actor. It was the first time he and his wife had spoken and posed for pictures since the birth of their baby daughter.

I found a crumpled skirt and jacket in one of my suitcases and an iron packed in another; a pair of tights, horribly laddered, but not anywhere visible once I was dressed, a pair of high heels separated in two different boxes. I closed my front door on the chaos and took a taxi to the Landmark Hotel on Marylebone Road. It was as straightforward a job as could be. A lovely family photograph, some gushing words about the new addition to the family, and a couple of amusing anecdotes about the birth.

'I thought it was a boy! And then the nurse told me I was looking at the umbilical cord!'

Actually, what he said was: 'It's a funny thing having a baby. You stop chasing your tail. All my life, I've been driven on by the question 'what next?' Now I feel complete. The emptiness has gone.'

A sculptor friend came to stay the following weekend. Before she left, she cleared out her workbag and among the bits of dry clay, old tissues and sweet wrappers she threw in my kitchen bin were a pair of ceramic baby feet. When she had gone, I retrieved the white footprints and studied the tiny curves left by pudgy toes and soft heels. And then, I couldn't throw them away again. I put them on the old university trunk at the end of my inflatable mattress. They comforted me. They were pure, white talismans to remind me what was important in life. I vowed I would stop wasting time on useless men and unhealthy relationships. When I went to sleep at night, I imagined they would miraculously guide me away from my corrupt, polluted life.

A month later I was sent to Russia to interview a serial killer.

3

The light from the fluorescent strips on Bratilov's landing bleached the faces of the guards waiting outside his cell on the top floor of the Bely Lebed Prison Colony.

Our boots stuck and clicked on the shiny brown linoleum as we moved down the corridor towards them.

A guard called out to Bratilov.

'He's telling him to stand against the wall,' whispered Olga.

Inside cell number 17 stood a young, slim, dark-haired man, his hands clasped behind his back, offering themselves up to the handcuffs.

When they were safely on, he was spun around and led out of the cell. His face was pale and translucent, as if it was years since he had felt the sun on it. His dark eyes gave no hint of the crimes he had committed or the hatred of women he had confessed in rages at prison psychiatrists.

Bratilov was taken into a small turquoise-coloured office and I watched from the doorway while two guards lowered him on to a small three-legged stool. They locked his hands behind him in silence. Olga and I sat behind a desk that separated us from him.

As he talked, the raised pink scar running across his throat wriggled into life. I watched the shape his lips made as his Russian words came tumbling out. I wondered if it was possible to see evil in the lines of his face. I listened carefully to the tone of his voice. Olga translated without his facial expressions. It was strange to hear his wicked words coming from her mouth.

'I only took off her clothes after I had strangled her,' repeated Olga's voice.

'I did something very wrong, and now I must suffer for it.'

He listed the names of the dead girls, like a roll-call, describing what he had done to each. He suddenly stopped.

'I would rather not go on,' he said in a whisper. His chin drooped against his chest.

'He says he would rather not go on,' repeated Olga in English.

Boris lit a cigarette for him, gently placed it in his mouth, and pushed an ashtray towards him across the table. Bratilov smoked it without the use of his hands, gulping like a fish through the side of his mouth. Occasionally, he tapped the ash off the end against the ashtray with a jerk of his head as if he was taking part in a bizarre party game.

When he had smoked it down to the filter, Boris removed it and ground it out.

Bratilov's face remained blank. He began speaking again, more confidently than before.

'I don't believe in free sex. All women are sluts and whores,' he said monotonously. 'I don't appreciate girls who just say,

"Today I will be with this one and tomorrow I will be with this one." A woman should only have sex with her husband.'

He fixed his soulless black eyes on me. I looked past him towards Lieutenant Valinsky at the back of the room.

The look on his face made me think of excitement and adventure. It made me feel as if I was searching for something. He made me want to run away through the snow into the forests of silver birches and pines – and keep running until I found it.

I wondered what it would be like to kiss him.

He smiled at me.

I felt heat rush to my cheeks and my head began to spin. But this time, I didn't return his smile because I didn't want Bratilov to see it.

We stayed at the prison to eat. Boris took us to a small dining room and brought us bread, soup and chicken. At a separate table, Lieutenant Valinsky sat gazing silently out of the window towards the forest. He looked serene, unshakeable, as if he didn't have a care in the world.

I asked Boris why he was sitting alone.

'There's more room for us without him,' he laughed mischievously.

'Couldn't we push our two tables together?' I asked. Olga translated.

Boris shrugged.

'Oh, he's fine over there,' he said, before calling to him. 'The *Anglichanka* is worried that you're on your own.'

He laughed softly, thanked me in English with a polite nod, and carried on eating.

Olga nudged me under the table and smiled.

'Be careful what you say, Barbara,' she said. 'I think your lieutenant is understanding more than he is letting on.'

I looked over towards his composed, gentle face, wondering if he could be guilty of such deceit.

I asked her: 'Who is he?'

'I have no idea,' she said. 'But don't you think it's strange that he suddenly turned up when we were looking through Bratilov's files? Maybe he's been sent to spy on us.'

We sniggered behind our hands, and Boris asked her why we were laughing. She shrugged and told him: 'Nichevo'.

Nothing.

* * *

Olga and I first met in Ukraine, three months before our trip to Russia. I had been sent from London to write a piece about the official closure of the Chernobyl nuclear power station and Olga, who worked for a British news agency in Moscow, was my translator. We arranged to meet in the foyer of Hotel Dnipro in Kiev. She was waiting for me when I stepped through the doorway, out of the snow and the inky-blue night. Her tiny frame was wrapped in a coat with a big fur hood. Her long dark plait trailed down her back.

'We'll save money. We'll share a room,' she said to me.

During the day, we stomped around in the snow interviewing stubborn families who refused to leave the poisonous dead zone around the infamous Chernobyl nuclear plant.

At night, in our hotel, we shared blinis, caviar and secrets with the easy familiarity of those who know they will probably never meet again.

I told her about Mr B. She told me that she didn't know her father. He had abandoned her mother when Olga was a child, and lived somewhere in Moscow with his new family.

She was the most serious and earnest twenty-three-year-old I had ever met. Nothing frightened her. She trusted no one, and expected nothing from anyone. Her mother and grandmother had lost everything when the rouble crashed in 1995.

'When my grandfather died he left enough in the bank for three cars,' she told me bitterly. 'That money was meant to be my inheritance.'

Olga didn't trust banks or roubles any more. She insisted her British boss paid her in pound sterling. Beneath her bed at home was a box filled with twenty-pound notes.

* * *

After lunch, we stepped outside the prison into the deathly cold of the Ural Mountains. It was minus thirty degrees, and my nose and eyes itched as we said goodbye to Boris at the main gate. Back at the Hotel Solikamsk in the centre of town, I took off my heavy, snow-damp boots and lay down on the bed.

Drifts of snow had crept up from the ledge to the panes, almost covering the glass. They muffled the noise of the traffic at the crossroads outside and cast a milky-white glow into the room. The silence and the light felt soft and dream-like. I stretched my arms across the shiny turquoise satin cover and remembered how I had recoiled in horror when I first saw the grey concrete 1950s block perched on the edge of Revolution Square. I didn't tell Olga for fear of spoiling the cultural blow she had struck against the diehard Soviet sitting in the lobby downstairs.

She had successfully browbeaten the woman on the front desk into admitting that the empty hotel did in fact have rooms to rent and, at the same time, had the satisfaction of confirming her belief that all Russians living anywhere but Moscow or St Petersburg were slightly backward.

'It's completely crazy,' she said. 'They would prefer to have a hotel with no guests than give a room to a foreigner. I can't believe how stupid these people are. They're so used to being suspicious of anyone who is not Russian. Can you imagine her face when I told her you were English?'

I saw for myself when I stepped inside. It was a look of both fear and wonder, the kind you might reserve for someone from another planet. She asked for my passport without looking at me, examined the photograph and visa without raising her eyes, and then copied my details on to a piece of shiny grey paper.

When she had finished writing, she handed my passport back and snatched a nervous look at me when she thought I couldn't see. I placed some roubles on the counter as a deposit, picked up a large key, and started up the three flights of shiny stone stairs leading to the top floor, feeling the woman's eyes following my ascent.

'It's a luxury apartment, built for Communist Party chiefs visiting the local magnesium plant,' Olga had enthused, her long dark plait bouncing in time with her steps.

'We even have our own bathrooms.'

The door had opened on to a horror scene from the 1970s. Strip lights cast a harsh glare over the yellow wallpaper, bright orange teak furniture and brown linoleum floor. Electric sockets dangled loosely out of the wall, emitting flashes of violet when anything was plugged in. Above them, '220 v' had been crudely scrawled in rusty red paint on the walls. The writing had dripped. It looked like blood.

The large dining room was dominated by a long black table surrounded by ten chairs. A matching glass-fronted cabinet was filled with silver and burgundy china and perfectly spaced iodine-coloured glasses.

A broken cassette player lay on its side in the corner. Dusty decorations, left over from the New Year celebrations a month earlier, looped across the ceiling. It was like arriving at a party long after the other guests had gone home.

Three bedrooms led off from a long corridor lined with a threadbare runner and pots of African violets. I took the first, Olga chose the second. We left the smallest room for Chris, who arrived a day after us.

Boris had been delighted when Olga told him a male photographer from London would be joining us. Apparently he'd heard that English girls weren't much good at drinking vodka.

* * *

A large bottle glistened menacingly on the table in Boris's office.

'Don't do it! It's a terrible drink, Barbara,' said Olga.

But Boris's words had started something. While he went to a cabinet to fetch some glasses, I felt my competitive streak rippling into life.

Lieutenant Valinsky arrived. He walked into the room

clasping several grey paper packages. He was very tall and slim, and still devastatingly handsome in his uniform.

I wondered what it would be like to feel his arms around me.

When everyone moved towards the table, I quickly slid into the seat next to his, beaming up at him shamelessly. He unwrapped the speckled paper revealing five dried orange fish with gaping mouths, a bunch of spring onions, some grey bread and a large white, greasy slab.

He took a knife from his pocket, flicked it open, and began cutting the white substance with large, smooth hands.

'It's *salo*. Raw pork fat,' enthused Olga, popping a piece in her mouth. 'It's better than you can get even in Moscow. Taste it! It melts on your tongue like chocolate.'

Lieutenant Valinsky held the plate towards me and nodded encouragingly. I gazed at him and ate.

The vodka drinking began. It seemed like a good idea at first.

Boris showed us how to gulp the contents of the shot glasses in one go. He exhaled with a sigh as he returned his glass to the table.

In between shots, the lieutenant explained, it was important to eat something – a slice of bread, a piece of salt fish. That way, you didn't get drunk.

He took a small square of bread and placed a piece of fish on it.

'Small sandweedge,' he said, urging me to eat. It was hard to communicate with him. He spoke a tiny amount of English, while my knowledge of Russian was virtually non-existent.

Each time he refilled my glass, he would tilt his head

slightly to one side and raise an eyebrow to ask if I wanted to continue.

The first few burnt my throat, but I nodded eagerly every time, feeling the warm, clear liquor charging through my veins.

Boris told stories, holding up his hand to silence us and calling us to attention with the announcement: 'Anecdote, anecdote!'

Olga translated his wild tales: Boris and his friends capturing and eating a wild dog when they had been sent on a survival exercise deep in the forest without any food; Lieutenant Valinsky finding himself face-to-face with a knife-wielding escaped convict while staying at an army training camp and wrestling him to the ground.

I wasn't sure if the weakness in my legs was the effect of the lieutenant sitting next to me, or the vodka I had drunk. Heat spread through my limbs.

I looked at him beside me. He appeared totally sober – as calm and serene as he was when I had first seen him. My drunken eyes moved slowly, and he caught me staring at him for what felt like the hundredth time that day. He stared back long and hard as if he was challenging me to admit it and when I conceded with a tired, resigned smile, he winked.

We left Boris's office just after midnight. Lieutenant Valinsky offered me his arm. I took it, looked up at him and sighed. 'You really are very beautiful,' I said.

He squeezed his arm against my hand.

'Can you understand what I'm saying?' I said in English, slurring my words.

He smiled and squeezed my hand again. I tried to

remember how many times I had told him how lovely he was. I laughed drunkenly.

'I don't care if you understand, I don't care. I don't care.'

He led me through the corridors. My feet moved, but I had no sense of where I was walking. My eyes were closed, my head rested against his arm. A blast of cold air told me we were outside. While I swayed in front of him, he flipped the collar of my coat up towards my ears and steered me into the army van with the others. We set off back towards town, via a twenty-four-hour pavement kiosk where a fur-gloved hand reached out to take Boris's money and pass him a bottle of vodka. I groaned at the sight of it.

For me, at least, the evening was over. Back at the Hotel Solikamsk, the lieutenant and the others sat around the big black table while Chris got glasses from the cabinet. I waved goodbye across the room and left them sitting among the colourful paper chains and green and red foil snowflakes.

I staggered into my room and fell straight on to the bed, exhausted and terribly drunk. The ceiling began spinning above me and my ears hummed and whined.

From across the corridor came the happy noise of friendships being forged. Then, through the sounds of muffled chat and laughter, sleep descended.

* * *

I woke to find myself face-to-face with a shiny brown cockroach sitting on the corner of the bedside table, waving its antennae disapprovingly at me.

I thought about Olga's warning the night before. I felt

terrible. I wished I was dead. Even the sight of the large insect, peering back at me, failed to jolt me out of my stupor.

I dragged myself out of bed, staggered into the tiny bathroom, fell to my knees on the stained, cracked floor tiles and threw up. The clothes I'd been wearing the day before clung to my damp skin. I peeled them off and smelt alcohol seeping from every pore. I turned on the taps and icy water spluttered into the blue plastic sink. I splashed some on my face, but it made my head ache even more. I felt sick to the pit of my stomach. I put on a t-shirt and lay down on the bed again.

Olga knocked on my door at seven and came in. She looked as neat and bright as ever. Not a hair in her long dark plait was out of place. She'd even managed to paint her nails a lurid metallic purple colour.

'Time to get up,' she said breezily.

'Olga,' I moaned from beneath the covers. 'I've poisoned myself. I'm dying. Help me.'

'Oh, Barbara,' she said, tutting. 'I tried to warn you. The men carried on until four this morning. I can't wake Chris up.'

I asked what had happened to Boris and the lieutenant.

She laughed. 'They went straight back to work, of course. They were absolutely fine.'

In the tiny, glossy turquoise blue kitchen, Olga inspected the gas cooker and immediately advised against its use.

'God knows if it's safe,' she said, staring at it suspiciously and shaking her head. 'We should just forget it. It's not worth the risk.'

We went out. In the lobby downstairs, Mrs Soviet had informed us that there was nothing to eat and drink. The restaurant, she said, was closed during the day. No, she didn't have a kettle. If we wanted something, there was a cafe near the bus station.

I followed Olga across the icy pavements, copying the safe, flat-footed, steady way she walked on the impacted snow without bending her legs. We arrived at an unmarked building. She pushed at a big rusting iron door that announced our entrance with a squeal as it scraped over the stone floor.

Men crowded around three round plastic tables fell silent and turned their heads as we walked in. Olga asked for coffee, and a waitress dressed in a pink and white frilly nylon uniform bobbed down behind the glass and popped up again, clasping two tiny plastic cups. She handed us one each, expressionless beneath her paper hat.

It was becoming increasingly obvious that it was impossible to read the faces of Russians. Even Olga stopped smiling when she spoke to her compatriots.

'It's true,' she said when I commented on it. 'If Russians see a stranger smiling at them, they know it's a foreigner.'

I peered inside the cup. A small spoonful of fine brown powder had been mixed with dried milk and lots of sugar. The frilly waitress pointed to a machine in the corner of the room, indicating that we had to add the hot water ourselves. When we had finished stirring, she demanded the tiny plastic spoons back.

4

When I was at school, Russia was the green canvas folder which carried my history notes; my creased, battered Penguin copy of *The Communist Manifesto*; the crowds of people running down the Odessa steps in Eisenstein's *Battleship Potemkin*; the black and white photograph inside the cover of my history text book showing Lenin with his pointed beard and small round spectacles standing on a podium and jabbing his pointed finger at the crowds in front of him.

Three times a week, inside the small, elevated prefab huts in the middle of the playground, my teacher would attempt to draw us into the vast mysterious grey world of the Soviet Union, standing in front of the blackboard and writing key words in thick white chalk: Bolshevik, Menshevik, the Provisional Government, the Purges, Collectivisation, the New Economic Plan, the Five Year Plans.

Miss Chapman, with her neat grey hair and miniature silver fifty-pence-piece earrings, would dramatically underline The Red Terror, The Red Army, unaware of the chalk dust floating down on to her right shoulder.

Russia was society gone wrong. Russia was what happens when those with political aspirations try and mould humanity to fit their own ideology.

Overriding everything was the image I had in my mind of Trotsky lying dead in the blood-stained snow, an ice-pick firmly embedded in his head.

My Russia seemed so far-fetched that for a long time I had no real geographical sense of the country at all. When I was fourteen, I carried a letter home from school to my parents, asking if they wanted me to go on a skiing trip to a resort near St Petersburg. The next day, having checked that my best friend was also going, I went back to school with a signed form and a deposit for fifty pounds.

At break-time, those going on the trip tried to out-do each other with fantastic tales from behind the Iron Curtain. One girl told how you could pack your case with Levi's jeans and sell them for a fortune on the streets in Moscow. Another warned that our hotel rooms would be bugged and anyone saying a bad word about the Government would be arrested and sent off to the Siberian salt mines.

But what would have been my first visit to Russia never transpired. A subtle shift in the ever-delicate relations between East and West in the 1980s meant that visas for the trip were out of the question. A letter of explanation and my father's cheque for fifty pounds was sent home, and so Russia remained as much of a mystery as ever.

Four years later at university in Oxford, I was drawn in a little further. Twice a week, I crossed the college gardens and knocked on the door of my history tutor's study. Inside, I'd pick my way across stray books and files and reams of paper towards an old green threadbare armchair.

Above the fireplace hung a huge red and gold hammer and sickle flag he had brought back from one of his many visits to the Soviet Union. He poured glasses of *Stolichnaya* vodka and placed an empty wine bottle between us for an endless stream of cigarettes. Georgian music played in the background as I read out my essays and he criticised them between mouthfuls of chocolate-covered ginger biscuits.

Why were there revolutions in Russia in 1917, and what was their character? How far were Collectivisation and the Purges an inevitable consequence of Bolshevism? Is Stalinism better seen as a corruption or as an extension of Leninism?

Towards the end of our tutorials, he made coffee in a teapot and didn't bother to strain it for grounds.

Russia left a gritty, bitter taste in the mouth and scratchy, smoke-sore eyes.

For three years, I read and I argued. I wrote about how the theory of Marxism was twisted and distorted by those in power, how communist leaders took Russia to the very place they had been trying to escape from. From my naive academic pedestal, I thought my arguments were sophisticated. I believed I understood Russians better than they understood themselves.

I was wrong. Russia could see right through me.

* * *

In Revolution Square it was still snowing. Men and women, buried in fur coats and hats, shuffled across the icy pavements. Mothers pushed babies in prams constructed on sledge runners.

Battered Lada cars sitting at traffic lights pumped out thick black smoke. Grey buses with passengers silhouetted behind ice-covered windows rattled by in front of us.

Olga jumped on and off the crumbling kerb, trying to flag down passing cars.

I asked her if she really thought one would stop.

'Of course,' she said, surprised that I should ask such a question. 'People are grateful for the chance to earn some money.'

'But is it safe?' I asked, perturbed at the thought of getting into a stranger's car.

She replied, 'I think so,' with a thoughtful frown, as if it was something she had never considered.

Sure enough, within minutes, a dull red 1970s Moskvich car pulled over. Olga leaned in through the open front passenger window and negotiated a price with its young driver.

'It's one dollar,' she called over her shoulder, before jumping in.

The road to the prison took us past the giant bell tower of Solikamsk's Trinity Cathedral, over the river, alongside the market where women wrapped in furs and headscarves sold knitted shawls and socks.

On the edge of the town, rows of grey, faceless Soviet apartment blocks merged into single-storey tsarist-era wooden dachas with ornately decorated window frames.

Finally, we turned off the main road down a dirt track and saw the towering blue-grey granite walls, the last man-made structure before Solikamsk faded into hundreds of miles of pine forests and then the mountains beyond.

*

Boris was in his office, looking for the addresses of the families of Bratilov's victims. Lieutenant Valinsky made me a cup of instant coffee. He stirred it carefully as he walked across the room.

'You feel bad after vodka?' he asked gently in English.

'Da, da, da,' I replied with a sigh.

He looked unaffected by lack of sleep or alcohol. He had changed out of his formal uniform and put on camouflage fatigues. The only telltale sign that he hadn't been to bed that night was his slightly ruffled black hair.

I leant my head against the cold stone wall and tried to shut out the waves of nausea welling up inside me.

He placed his hand gently on my arm and led me to a chair. Once again, I fought the urge to lean against him.

* * *

A group of officers had arrived from the city of Perm, about five hours' drive from Solikamsk. Cannibal killers, it transpired, were not such a rarity after all. The Perm officers were investigating another one and had come to compare notes. Such a happy occasion meant more vodka drinking – a terrifying prospect in itself but, more importantly, an excuse to spend more time with Lieutenant Valinsky.

We were shown into the office of the head of the prison, Major Vladimir Tyshchenko. 'Barbara, Barbara, Barbara!' he said in a 'what-are-we-going-to-do-with-you' tone of voice. He was a tall, powerfully built man with cropped, fair, curly hair and a deep voice.

It was strange to see him smiling. The first time I had met

him he had shouted at Olga and glared at me, furious at the presence of two 'busybodies' in his prison.

Now, having heard about my courageous bid to take on the Russians at their national pastime, he looked at me like an indulgent father.

'Vodka?' he teased, holding the bottle above my glass.

I told him: 'Nyet vodka. Nyet, nyet, nyet.'

He sat next to me and I asked him where Lieutenant Valinsky was.

'Dima!' he bellowed, using the shortened version of his name. A muffled, softer voice called back from the room next door.

'The *Anglichanka* wants you,' called the Major.

He pretended to introduce us:

'Barbara . . . Dima!'

He sat down so close to me that our legs were touching.

'You look for me?' he asked.

'Yes,' I said. I didn't feel the need to give an explanation. Neither did he expect one.

'No problem,' he said softly.

The party was in full flow when the door to Boris's office was flung open and two young women dressed from head to foot in mink stormed in like raging bears. Only their angry white faces were visible beneath fur. One was tall, thin and stony-faced. The other was shorter and rounder. Jagged blonde hair fell from beneath her fur hat as she stepped forward and began screaming at Boris. Her shrill voice and glittering blue eyes silenced the room. Boris's mischievous face crumbled into a boyish grimace, and he bowed his head in shame.

'I think she is to kill him,' Dima whispered, drawing his hand across his throat.

The men cheered as his giant, gawky frame was dragged from the room by his tiny wife. Before she left, she threw a menacing look over her shoulder, narrowing her accusing eyes first at a giggling Olga, then at me, before sniffing the air and turning on her heel.

The door slammed behind her, rattling the table and the vodka glasses on it. Everyone laughed, although for most of the men it was in relief that it hadn't been their own ferocious wives coming to claim them.

When the vodka ran out we returned to our apartment in the same khaki jeep and via the same all-night vodka kiosk. The party continued around the black table. Olga and I took out the iodine-coloured glasses from the cabinet and brought slices of bread and pork from the kitchen.

'And now we fight,' said the Major, rolling up his sleeves and turning to Chris, who stepped backwards from his towering frame.

Olga explained it was a sign of friendship. 'Only when you have fought can you really be brothers.'

The Major settled for arm-wrestling and slammed Chris's forearm on to the table. Dima took his place and did the same. So too, to Chris's shame, did their pale, spotty, rather scrawny-looking driver.

The men exchanged gifts as a sign of their respect. The Major's leaf-shaped silver lighter and old Soviet dog tags were swapped with Chris's favourite pen.

'If anything ever happens to you,' said the Major, 'I will

find out about it wherever you are in the world.

They hugged with tears in their eyes.

In this intoxicating mood of friendship, we reminisced fondly about the Second World War when our countries shared a common enemy. We blamed the former hostility and suspicion between East and West on the political machinations of government, as if the Cold War had been a minor squabble in a long and happy love affair. Governments aside, we declared, the Russian and the British people were natural friends and allies.

We discussed world politics, the cost of living in our respective countries, the different roles of men and women, our families, children. Vast amounts of vodka were knocked back in the small yellow-tinted shot glasses, and layers of cigarette smoke curled around the room.

When the vodka ran out, Chris produced a fifty-dollar note to buy more, and our Russian friends scoffed and threw it back at him. Eventually, the Major set the offending piece of paper alight, despite the fact that it amounted to half his monthly salary.

London seemed far away. Thousands of miles from home, in our cockroach-ridden apartment, I felt happier than I could remember being for a long time.

We toasted each other again and again.

'To our two nations, to world peace, to friendship, to love.'

I was sitting around a table with people whose language I didn't speak, and believed I had stumbled across the essence of humanity.

At the heart of it was Dima – my beautiful lieutenant.

The Major lifted his glass again.

'To Dima and the *Anglichanka*,' he said.

He ordered us to drink. We cupped our arms and looped them through each other's. When we had drunk the vodka, Dima lent towards me swiftly and kissed me on the lips.

He stayed the night. No grand decisions were made. While Dima and I were making coffee in the kitchen, the Major and Boris hatched a plot to leave without him. They took their driver with them.

We walked hand-in-hand to my room and undressed without speaking. He left his uniform neatly folded on a chair in the corner before climbing into the bed and wrapping his arms around me.

In the morning, we stayed curled up in bed until thirst drove him to the kitchen and the bottles of cool beer inside what he called 'the big white box'.

5

From the moment we became lovers, we were a couple. I'd only been in Russia for ten days, but like a lovesick teenager, I couldn't bear to be apart from him and I couldn't see beyond him. He was twenty-eight – the same age as I was – and yet our lives had been played out in different worlds. The burden of choice was something he had never experienced. He had no goals or ambitions. His path through life had been dictated by necessity. At eighteen he began doing his National Service with the Red Army. Two years later he signed up, like his father before him, because the only alternative was working in one of the paper pulp factories in Solikamsk. He wasn't in pursuit of such mysteries as love or happiness or fulfilment. It would never have occurred to him to be so self-indulgent. He didn't struggle to better himself. He existed. He was a survivor.

When he sat next to me, I breathed him in. He smelt of tobacco, sweat and musky aftershave. I looked at him and saw salvation.

None of the others ever questioned it. Major Tyshchenko

thought it was romantic.

Boris thought it was hilarious. Olga was delighted at the prospect of my Russification. Even Chris behaved as if it was the most normal thing in the world.

A kind of madness had descended. Perhaps it was sanity. At first it was an overwhelming sense of energy surging through me. My senses were on fire. I could smell Russia in every breath: diesel fumes and stale tobacco smoke; wet gloss paint on corridors; the pungent aniseed of freshly chopped dill. They merged in every dizzy breath. When I inhaled I felt Russia pressing down, the weight of its vastness swirled around me.

There was the crisp, white light of the snow and the frozen, stinging air which pinched my skin. My body had come alive. I could feel again.

It was as if I had been sleepwalking and had suddenly woken up. I could see clearly for the first time. The decaying concrete buildings comforted me. Ambition and striving dissolved in their shadows.

London seemed like an insignificant, dark, sprawling mass on the other side of the world. In Solikamsk, I saw only survivors. I wondered what it would be like to merely exist as they did, without constantly questioning the past and worrying about the future.

I felt liberated, reckless and invincible.

Mother Russia had seduced me. She was going to save me from myself.

* * *

Our stay in Solikamsk was prolonged for several days by the weather. Relentless blizzards had descended across the Urals. It was as if time itself had been frozen. Interviews with the families of Bratilov's victims in a town five hours' drive away would have to wait.

Outside, the minus thirty-five degrees cold froze the inside of my nose and made every breath painful.

Inside the hotel, industrial-sized radiators belted out hot, claggy air day and night and cockroaches roamed the ceiling and walls. Sober, I couldn't bear them. Olga scoffed at my cowardice and joined me in my room for a roach hunt.

'You should see my flat in Moscow,' she told me, as she peered carefully behind the torn edges of wallpaper. 'It's a very old building and there are hundreds there.'

She told me about the time she put poison down for the insects lurking in the pipes and skirting boards.

'I came back from work and there were little bodies everywhere,' she said, revelling in the look of disgust on my face.

The Solikamsk cockroaches came in all different colours and sizes. I found a blue one and even Olga was impressed. I fantasised that it was a super-Soviet breed that had evolved in the depths of one of the town's factories. But it was mortal enough to die in the same way as the others, with several weighty blows from one of my boots.

There was still no hot water. Every day since we had arrived, Mrs Soviet on the reception desk had promised it would be fixed, and every night the building would groan with the ghostly shrieks of air being forced through pipes, and the sound of a hammer striking metal resounded through the walls.

'Oh Barbara! It will never get mended!' Olga said cheerfully when I moaned about it. She soon taught me to lower my expectations.

'Only then,' she advised me, 'will you be like a real Russian woman.'

I learned quickly. Without hope, it is surprising how content you can be.

Dima didn't notice the squalor in our ten-dollar-a-night apartment. He was seemingly oblivious to the freezing water, the peeling wallpaper and the cockroach nests, and when I waited for him to return to the apartment in the evening, so was I.

He came every evening without fail. As with everything, we never discussed it – he just always came. Between seven and eight o'clock, I would feel sick with blissful anticipation – a condition deliciously alleviated by his knock on the door.

I would jump up eagerly to let him in, and happily notice how the flakes of snow nestling in his fur had not melted in the time it had taken him to run up the three flights of stairs.

Major Tyshchenko decided we should get married.

'He needs a good woman in his life,' he told Olga, who translated in turn when he and Boris visited one evening.

'He is a good man. A very deep thinker. He loves philosophy and yoga and the spiritual life.'

'Dima and Barbara should get married, and their first-born son can be Peter after Peter the Great.'

Olga agreed that it was a wonderful idea.

'You can come and live in Russia,' she said.

'He needs to get divorced first,' interrupted Boris with a smile.

As a favour to him, Dima had married Boris's younger sister Larissa a year earlier to help get her an apartment. It was a common scam in towns like Solikamsk where severe housing shortages meant you could spend decades on a waiting list. With no money to build new homes, the municipal property committee grappled with the thousands of names jostling for attention on lists. Young married couples were among those often lucky enough to jump the queue.

While procedure demanded that couples usually had to wait at least two months after declaring their desire to be wed, with the help of a few roubles, Boris managed to persuade the ZAGS (the Russian registry office) official at the town hall that Dima and Larissa were so in love they couldn't possibly survive that long.

On the agreed date of their wedding, Dima had slipped out of the apartment he shared with his mother, telling her he was going to meet friends, and walked to the ZAGS registry office.

After they had exchanged vows and signed their names, they kissed for the first and last time and were about to go their separate ways when a photographer from the local newspaper, the *Solikamsk Rabochiy*, stopped them.

'You are such a good-looking couple,' he told Dima and Larissa. 'Can I take your picture for the newspaper?'

They politely refused.

'Can you imagine what my mother would have said if our picture had appeared?' Dima groaned when he told us about it. 'I think she would have killed me.'

Eventually of course, Dima's mother found out. The family name, Valinsky, was uncommon, and before too long word reached her that a young woman in the town had re-styled herself 'Valinskaya' – the Russian equivalent of Mrs Valinsky. She was furious and didn't speak to Dima for a month.

Even before the marriage scam with Larissa, Dima had experienced matrimonial life. His girlfriend Tanya had fallen pregnant when she was nineteen and he was twenty. They were marched to the registry office by her parents, and stayed together until their daughter Yulia was four.

He showed me a picture of Yulia. She had chestnut eyes and a big white bow in her auburn hair. She clutched a toy dog on her lap.

'She is to be eight now,' he said. 'But I am not looking at her for three years.'

We left the apartment to buy more vodka. His leather jacket creaked as we walked along the grey icy pavements in the darkness, and our frozen breath shimmered in front of us. He put his fur hat on my head and placed one of my gloveless hands in his pocket with his. When we reached the shop, I reluctantly removed it so he could take out his money.

On the way back, we passed a statue of Lenin. His arm was outstretched, his finger pointing.

'Look,' said Dima. 'Lenin is to show the way home.'

Back at the hotel, he stopped me in front of a mirror on the staircase. He stood behind me, his chin resting on the top of my head.

'It's to be you and me,' he said seriously at my reflection in the mirror, before leading me up the rest of the stairs.

He followed me into the kitchen when I went to get more beer from the fridge.

'Barbara. I very want to kiss you,' he said.

I turned, wrapped my arms around him and leant my forehead against his shoulder, dizzy with relief, recklessness and desire.

In bed that night, I ran my fingers over his silky smooth brown skin. It was tanned from summer fishing expeditions and river swimming. His body looked like the bare-chested statue of the Second World War hero in the town's Komsomol Square. Perfectly sculpted, strong, unmoveable. I lingered over every flaw: the scar that bit deep into his left shoulder, one which ran across the back of his hand, another above his eyebrow.

Each had a story. A knife wound from an escaped prisoner; a schoolboy fight; an ice hockey accident. He told his tales with pictures and words scribbled in my notebook. Sometimes we struggled to explain ourselves with Olga's Russian/English dictionary. Sometimes we gave up with shrugs and smiles.

His life story was etched on his body. So many adventures and yet, when he slept, his face was carefree and peaceful. He made me feel that if I stayed with him, I would never be afraid of anything ever again.

Early in the morning, when the sky outside was turning blue-black, he got dressed quietly and set off for the prison.

I listened to the hollow sound of the closing wooden door, footsteps fading along the corridor, and fought the urge to run after him.

I jumped out of bed towards the icy window and rubbed the frozen glass, waiting for him to emerge below. In the orange glow of the street lamps, I watched him making his way across Revolution Square. Just before he reached the corner he turned, looked up at the window and waved. Then he dropped his arm and turned back, continued walking and disappeared from sight.

* * *

Boris was in trouble. Having frog-marched him out of the prison, his angry wife had refused to let him out for the last three days.

We were sitting around a formica table in Solikamsk's only restaurant and Dima was telling Olga, Chris and I about Boris's ordeal.

When Boris had tried to explain to Yulia that the prison had English visitors who needed entertaining, she scoffed at him.

'I have listened to your lies for years,' she told him, 'but this has to be the most ridiculous yet.'

All the other tables in the hotel restaurant were empty. A giant disco ball hanging from the ceiling sprinkled us with flecks of silver light. Russian pop music blared out over the loud-speakers. It had been turned on as soon as we entered the room.

The orange-haired, heavily made-up woman who had taken our coats as we arrived reappeared at our table with menus.

'We only have chicken,' she said, 'So please don't ask for anything else.'

There wasn't anything to drink either – except orange squash.

Half an hour later the waitress reappeared, tottering

towards us on high heels. A frilly white apron now covered her smart black pencil skirt.

Her lipsticked mouth whispered in Olga's ear.

'Please come to the kitchen and look at the chicken. I'm not sure if it's cooked.'

While Olga was gone, Boris appeared. His wife had gone out for an hour and he had to get home before she did.

He had a pair of gold hoop earrings in a little plastic envelope. He held them up in the air with a cynical smile as if to say: 'These should do the trick.'

When we finished dinner, he said, he wanted us to call at his apartment. He was determined to present us to his wife as proof of his honesty, hoping no doubt that one big truth would disguise the white lies he so often told her.

'Make sure you bring the *Anglichanka* and her friends,' he said to Dima, before heading towards the door.

Olga emerged from the kitchen carrying plates of blackened chicken. The orange-haired woman had already changed into a pair of overalls and was sweeping the floor.

Dima and I walked arm-in-arm through the white streets of Solikamsk to Boris's house. The night was freezing, dry and breathless, and our feet crunched on virgin snow as we walked in moonlight.

We moved slowly, falling behind Olga and Chris, and Dima softly sang an English pop song he had heard on the radio, asking me if I knew it.

'I turn to you,' he sang over and over again, while I shook my head in bemused ignorance.

'It is by Melanie of the Spice Girls.'

'Melanie B or Melanie C?' I asked. Dima didn't understand.

'Tell me please,' he continued. 'What does it mean, "I turn to you"?'

I mimed the gesture of turning, exaggeratedly twisting my shoulders as I swivelled in the snow.

'I . . . turn . . . to you.' I repeated the movements twice and he nodded his head and uttered a brief 'Mmm'.

I doubted that he was any the wiser, but he seemed satisfied with my explanation.

Away from the centre of Solikamsk, old wooden tsarist buildings with fairytale windows draped in sugary snow stood at the edge of the road. Behind them, row after row of bleak Soviet apartment blocks towered in rising grey tiers. Broken and subsided concrete steps cut through them leading to Boris's block.

Outside, two men sat smoking on an old broken wooden bench and stared as we walked past them into an unlit, dank stairwell.

Boris's honesty was rewarded with a kiss and a playfully pinched cheek by his wife, once she had heard English being spoken. His fantastic story was true. He had been vindicated. She took the gold hoop earrings out of their little plastic packet and put them on. She was pleased with him.

But she looked disapprovingly at my hand in Dima's before turning to Olga.

'What's the point in it all?' she said frowning. 'What on earth can come of it?'

I helped her lay the table with roast pork and potatoes and

frozen red berries picked in the forest by the Kapolev family and stored through the winter in a basket on their rickety balcony. Curiosity got the better of her and her face softened as she tried to speak to me in French.

'*Je ne parle pas anglais,*' she said, shrugging her shoulders and smiling at me for the first time. Peeping out from beneath her long bleached blonde fringe, I noticed how large her dark blue eyes were.

Despite the grim shell which housed them, Boris's DIY had transformed the flat inside. Gold-patterned paper covered the walls and a mahogany glass-fronted cabinet held crystal glasses and ornaments.

They had given the only room to their twelve-year-old daughter Katya, who slept on a narrow camp bed. On the wall at the end of it she had stuck a picture of Britney Spears, carefully cut out of a magazine. Her schoolbooks and clothes lay in neat piles on the floor.

Out came the vodka and the men began to drink. Olga looked on approvingly as I accepted Yulia's offer of tea.

'You are turning into a Russian woman, Barbara,' she said with satisfaction.

Vodka separated the men from the women. Yulia, Katya, Olga and I huddled around one side of the table, and I found myself following their example and throwing disapproving looks at Dima, Boris and Chris on the other.

They were looking at Boris's photographs from a recent tour of duty in Chechnya: Boris and his friends on a train heading south, playing cards and drinking vodka; in an army truck drinking vodka; on another train, stripped to their underwear inside the sweaty, airless carriage, arm-wrestling and drinking vodka; Boris lying on his belly behind a mound of sandbags, clutching a Kalashnikov rifle and a bottle of vodka.

He lifted up his t-shirt to show Chris a small tattoo across his rib cage. To outwit the enemy in case of his death, he had cunningly had his army number imprinted on his body so that he could be identified even if the Chechens wreaked their usual revenge and cut his head off. He drew his hand across his throat, laughing and baring his gold teeth. It didn't seem to bother him that in order to secure this little triumph, he would have to die first.

The following morning, after Dima had left for work, there was a knock at the apartment door.

It was Yulia and she was out of breath.

'None of the children believed Katya at school this morning when she told them she has English friends,' she said. 'You have to come with me.'

We went with her, determined to help her save Katya's reputation among staff and fellow pupils.

The English classroom at Solikamsk's School Number 1 was dominated by a large stern-looking portrait of the Queen hung on the wall and surrounded by photographs of other members of the Royal Family. Their names had been written in English on strips of paper and stuck underneath, but Prince Andrew and Edward had somehow got mixed up. There was a map of the United Kingdom and a set of postage stamps and the children were on their feet, singing in English.

'Mother's in the kitchen, father's in the garden . . .'

We clapped enthusiastically when they finished, and Katya's teacher asked Chris if he would say a few words to the class. He looked rather pleased. He walked to the front of the class and spoke to a sea of young faces gazing back in ignorance. They didn't understand a word he was saying, but when he finished they clapped anyway.

Minutes later we were frog-marched into the school hall, closely followed by the rest of the class. There were prizes to be given out.

'And to present them,' announced the Direktor, standing up in front of the rest of the school, 'we have two very special guests all the way from London in England.'

Katya smiled and waved from the back, before giving her friends an 'I-told-you-so' look.

Even so, Olga told me later that she had overheard two boys at the back of the hall saying: 'English people indeed! Really! These Muscovites must think we're completely stupid.'

6

Time was running out.

'What the hell are you doing out there?' asked my editor when I eventually called the office in London. We had only been away for two weeks, but his voice already seemed like a distant echo from another world. It was hard to know what to say to him. London didn't seem real any more. And I didn't want anything to do with it.

I didn't want to listen to his voice. I mumbled something about the weather holding us up, and cut him off.

When the Urals blizzards finally stopped, Chris, Olga and I set off for Lysva to find the families of Bratilov's victims and round up photographs of them for our article. Once we had left the orange glow of Solikamsk behind us, the road stretched out in front of us looked like the mottled grey and white surface of an ice rink after an evening of skating. The light of the full moon turned the vast swathes of snow blue. They rolled over the land as far as the eye could see.

The driver turned up the stereo and the tinny sound of trashy euro-music filled the car, wiping out the soft, white silence outside.

'It's so cold out there, take my hand and we'll be strong, on and on . . .'

Occasionally, he reached into the inside pocket of his rough twill jacket for a gold carton of cigarettes and opened the window to smoke, letting in blasts of icy air. Even with the heating on full, the cold seeped up through the floor and into my boots. I thought of the frozen road whizzing past just inches beneath me and tried to move my painful feet, but it hurt less to keep them still.

Olga, Chris and I were too tired to speak. Cloying diesel fumes made my head spin. I felt myself slipping towards sleep, aware that every muscle in my body was tensed as if somehow, through will-power alone, I could keep out the cold.

Bratilov's hunting ground, Pushkin Park, was deserted and quiet in the evening sunlight. The sky was as white as the snow covering the grass and trees. There was no breeze. Even the rusting Ferris wheel seemed frozen.

In the tidy first-floor flat of another grey apartment block, Sergiy Morozov, the father of fourteen-year-old Valentina, spat out his grief. He was flicking through a photograph album, holding it up every time he reached a picture of his pretty blonde daughter. Their faces were strikingly similar – father and daughter shared the same soft round nose and wide lips.

'The day I meet that monster will be the last day of his life,' he muttered. 'I can't believe he is allowed to live.'

Elena Lyzhina, who was blinded by Bratilov, lived in a flat on the opposite side of the same street. Her mother answered the door and showed us into a small, sparsely furnished sitting room. When Olga started gently questioning her, she wailed and placed her head in her hands. There was no question of taking her photograph.

We rounded up pictures of Bratilov's other victims from the offices of the local newspaper. It was late by the time Chris had copied them all and as the temperature plummeted, we looked for somewhere to stay for the night.

Olga ran into the first hotel we stopped at and returned to the car, saying that the heating had broken so all the rooms were freezing.

'I think we'll die if we stay there,' she said cheerily.

We found another hotel and huddled in its foyer eating fried chicken and potatoes. The constantly opening front door carried blasts of freezing air inside, but we had been forced out of the restaurant by the disco which had just started inside.

I thought of my empty bedroom in the apartment in Solikamsk and wondered what Dima was doing now. Before we left, he had given me his old Soviet dog tags and Red Army fur hat. I thrust my hand deep into my bag to feel them.

It was Saturday night, and Lysva's young men and women were heading to the town's only nightspot. Despite the cold, girls dressed in garish skimpy Lycra dresses with bare legs, heavy eye make-up and purple lipstick came striding through the front door on stilettos, spraying snow towards us.

Teenage boys in leather jackets and fur hats eyed them up and down hungrily, before closing in and following them into the restaurant where they were swallowed up by the din of Russian pop music.

'They look like prostitutes,' I said to Olga. 'How can they go out dressed like that?'

'They have to get a man,' she said. 'That's the whole purpose of the evening for them. A Russian girl needs to get married quickly or people will think that there's something wrong with her. And the easiest way to get married is to get pregnant first.'

Back in Moscow, where Olga was one of a new breed of modern Westernised career girls, neighbours stopped her in the street with looks of concern. Despite the fact that she was only twenty-four, they would tut disapprovingly: 'Still not married?'

When her single status dragged on, she explained, they speculated as to what the problem might be.

'Is it something gynaecological?' a middle-aged man asked Olga's mother one day. 'I have a very good doctor I can recommend. Do you want the number?'

On another occasion, Olga heard the elderly woman next door whispering to her daughter, while casting pitying looks at Olga as she passed along the landing of the apartment block.

'Such a shame.'

'Most Russian girls get married before they are twenty and then divorce,' said Olga.

I said I thought it was a very young age to be married.

'Oh the divorce rate is very high.' she admitted. 'But you see, it's perfectly respectable to be divorced. Most women can't put up with Russian men for very long anyway. It's the vodka.'

While we talked, the DJ changed records. Desperate, harsh voices echoed around the hotel. I had heard the same song several times since arriving in Russia. It was by the Moscow pop duo, Tatu. Olga laughed when I said I liked it because, she explained, the lyrics were about two teenage girls telling their parents they were in love with each other.

It was called *Ya Soshla S Uma* – 'I've lost my mind'. I smiled when Olga told me. Whenever I heard it, I wanted to run outside into the snow, throw my head back and scream.

As the song boomed out across the foyer, the realisation that I might have unleashed a life inside me hit me in a wave.

I imagined how it would feel to hold my baby. I could imagine the weight of it in my arms. And I wasn't afraid. I felt free.

Meeting Rita Butorskaya didn't frighten me either. Not even when she cupped her enormous stomach with a calloused hand. Or when she nodded her head towards the bedroom where her drunk husband lay snoring in the middle of the day in a vodka-induced stupor.

She was twenty-four years old and eight months pregnant. Her three-year-old son Pasha held on to a fold of her tatty cotton dress and stared curiously at Chris's camera. Since her tiny dacha had only one bedroom, her other son, six-year-old Gosha, now lived at his grandmother's.

'Twenty-four years old with three children . . .' said Chris in disbelief when Olga translated. 'Her life is over.'

It was our last day. Having listened to my weather excuses for days, my editor had asked for an article about what it was like to live in one of the coldest inhabited places on earth, before we set off back to Moscow and then London.

'Cold! Pah!' said Boris when Olga explained. 'You English don't know the meaning of cold.'

He would take us, he boasted, to a village where electricity was virtually unheard of and where the only water came from a spring at the edge of the forest.

When we arrived, Belkino, a scattering of small wooden houses, was barely visible.

It had barely been touched by the wars, revolutions and famines that had raged around it over the last century.

A river of snow had covered the road, cutting the village in half. It seemed deserted except for two wolf-like dogs wading through the drifts. Their legs weren't visible.

Rita's wooden house was the first we came to. She was milking a cow in a shed built on to the back, and didn't hear Boris knocking at first. After inviting us in, she took off her coat and hat and the grey felt *valenki* she wore on her feet.

A giant stone wood-fired oven at the centre of the room belted out heat. On top of it were piles of old blankets, baskets of berries and onions, and buckets of potatoes.

'When the baby comes in a month,' she said, 'I'm hoping it's going to be a girl.'

She glanced bitterly towards the bedroom door, from where her husband's drunken snores could be heard, and tightened her lips.

'Of course, he doesn't care what it will be.' she added.

'He doesn't care about anything. He lost his job. He spends his days fishing now.'

If her 'Russian Man' was sober enough to take her, Rita planned to give birth at the hospital in the nearest town, Berezniki, about an hour's drive away.

I found it hard to stop staring at her. I wondered what it would be like to struggle as she did, but for something real.

Beneath her roughly cropped hair, large brown eyes stared out from flawless, milky skin. Her lips were as pink as a child's. There was something innocent and pure about her. Uncorrupted.

Chris was showing Pasha a photograph of himself on the screen at the back of his digital camera.

'He has never had his photograph taken before,' Rita told Olga.

Rita placed her hand on his shining blond hair and smiled at his reaction. There was purpose and love in her pale, exhausted face.

I pictured Dima and I living in a snow-covered dacha like Rita's, sleeping on a bed covered in animal fur. Dima at work while I pickled cucumbers, baked loaves of grey bread, and dried berries and onions. Dima bringing home wood for the fire and meat for us to eat. Dima striding through the heavy, padded, insulated front door at night, stepping into the oven-cosy warmth inside, taking off his military hat and encircling me with his arms. Dima stepping out into the frozen garden to lower joints of pork into an ice-hole. I pictured Dima and I lying in bed at night, listening to the wind and snow raging outside, safe beneath a quilt of animal furs.

I saw myself pregnant like Rita, in the late summer when the earth was warm and moist, picking mushrooms in the forest. Dima telling me off for overdoing it and insisting on carrying the buckets of water from the spring at the end of the village. Dima holding our baby in his arms. The three of us together.

I wanted to be with him so badly, I could no longer see beyond him. I wanted to live another life.

*

A fresh layer of snow had already covered our tracks when we trudged back to the army van which Boris had commandeered for the day.

We drove back towards Solikamsk and I thought of Dima with the same hungry anticipation I always felt before seeing him.

He was waiting at the prison gates when we arrived to collect him, and he climbed into the van and pulled me towards him and into his grey fur-collared army coat. His cheek felt cold against my face. I could smell the cigarette he had just smoked on his warm breath.

He smiled at me in the darkness as the van set off again, and I imagined for a terrifying minute what it would be like to go back to London and carry on with my life as before. I wondered what I could do to stop it.

* * *

At a large dacha on the edge of Solikamsk, another of Dima and Boris's friends was preparing a small farewell party for us.

We had been in Russia for nearly three weeks, and the following morning we would drive to Perm airport and fly home.

Ivan and his rosy-cheeked wife, Nina, had prepared a table covered in roasted pork and chicken, bowls of boiled potatoes smothered in homemade sour cream and sprinkled with dill and *pelmeni* – Siberian dumplings filled with meat.

'I have a good wife,' said Ivan, proudly kissing her. Her ruddy face blushed an even deeper shade of pink and she went to the kitchen to fetch bottles of beer for the men.

'A good marriage is the most important thing in your life if you want to be happy and healthy,' added Fidel, the mustachioed driver who had taken us to Belkino. He raised his glass and the men drank a toast to the women, raising their glasses to Nina, Olga and I as representatives of our feted sex.

Ivan stood up. 'You should marry the *Anglichanka*,' he said to Dima. 'Your life will be better for it.'

'But maybe not Barbara's life,' quipped Olga, and she and Nina raised their eyebrows at each other.

Dima cursed at them under his breath and put his arm around me.

'Don't listen to them,' he said. 'It's a very bad joke.'

Fidel stared into his glass and then looked around the table.

'I would like to drink a toast to my beautiful wife,' he said in a most unRussian Man manner.

'She is always smiling when I come home from work. She is a good mother. She never complains. I couldn't ask for more from her.'

His voice trembled with emotion as he spoke and when he raised his glass to his absent wife, his eyes were moist with tears.

Several drinks later, Ivan and Fidel moved the furniture to the sides of the small living room, put on some music and started dancing. Ivan made great galloping movements as he swung his bulky frame from side to side with his hands extended above his head.

Olga, Chris, Dima and I joined him, crashing into the furniture as the men took it in turns to twirl the girls around the room.

When Fidel found Olga at his side, he lifted her up, but didn't put her down again. When he tried to kiss her, she pushed him away in horror so that he dropped her awkwardly. She paced across the room towards me.

'So much for his perfect wife,' she muttered, her face taut with anger.

Dima and I slipped away from the others. Nina had fired up the banya, the steam room in a wooden hut at the bottom of their garden, and we decided to take our turn first.

We undressed in the bedroom, and Dima carefully turned me around and took off the silver cross around my neck. In robes and flip-flops, we set off outside along a gully ploughed through the snow leading to the banya.

After the freezing cold, the heat was shocking. We washed each other's hair with hot water from a tank inside, and when the temperature became unbearable I tried to open the door, desperate to escape it.

'Nyet, nyet,' said Dima, sniffing exaggeratedly to show me what would happen if I let the cold air in.

Even so, when we were dripping in steam and sweat, he flung open the door and we ran outside and jumped in the snow laughing and shrieking.

'I want to be pregnant,' I told him.

At first he didn't understand.

'I want to have a baby.' I said. 'I want to have your baby.'

His eyes widened as my meaning dawned. 'In nine months?' he said, amazed.

'Yes', I replied with a serious face. Tears slid silently from my eyes. Dima threw back his head and laughed before looking back at me with a straight face.

'OK,' he said gently, taking my hands in his.

We stayed at Ivan's that night. I slept fitfully with Dima on a sofa bed in the living room, feeling every hour slip past away from me and out of reach.

When morning came, I held on to him and cried like a love-sick teenager.

My head felt swollen from the vodka I had drunk the night before and I woke to the sound of Fidel's voice calling out Dima's name. At 6 a.m. he opened the door and shouted at him to hurry up and get in the van that was waiting outside.

'Dima nyet!' I shouted back at him, grabbing Dima's arm.

I was behaving like a hysterical adolescent. I could feel the panic rising up into my throat. It was the last time I would see him. Dima was leaving for the prison and in a few hours I would set off on the journey home. It was over. As easily as I had slipped into his life, so I would slip out of it again, back to Moscow and then London.

My head reeled at the thought of my life: the rush-hour drive to the office, picture-perfect supermarket food, my constantly ringing mobile phone, junk mail interspersed with letters from the bank, fear of failure, fear of meaninglessness. A constant onward march towards a perfect life that I knew would always stay out of reach.

Dima dressed quickly and firmly wiped the tears from my eyes with both his thumbs. We kissed slowly, he turned and hurried out of the door.

It slammed behind him, and reality hit me in a brutal wave. My Russian lieutenant had gone. It was finished.

The sun came up. It was brilliant and harsh. I stood outside Ivan's wooden house, my feet entrenched in the deep snow, and smoked a cigarette from the golden packet Dima had left behind. The whiteness was blinding against the bright turquoise sky. It made my eyes water to look at it. I knew I couldn't go back to my old life. It was too late.

Something had changed.

7

In London, I opened the front door of my flat to find Bratilov staring up at me from the floor.

Our interview had been published on 13 February – my last evening with Dima – and three copies of the newspaper lay on the doormat, alongside the bank statements, credit card bills and a speeding fine, awaiting my return. Bratilov and I had been honoured with a position on the front page.

It was billed as 'The year's most terrifying interview', and a photograph of the two of us talking had been superimposed across a grossly magnified image of his eyes.

All I could think about was what the picture didn't show. It didn't show Dima, Boris and Vladimir, who were standing behind Chris when he took the photograph. It didn't show Olga, translating at my side. It was like staring through a doorway to another world, unable to walk through it and see around the corners.

I put down my bags in the hallway and breathed in the familiar smell of home. It was silent except for the sound of the fridge. Everything was exactly as I had left it three weeks earlier when I set off for Heathrow to get a flight to Moscow.

The duvet lay half on, half off the bed: exactly where I had thrown it when the alarm went off at 5 a.m. My pyjamas lay screwed up in a heap on the floor. A half-empty cup of black coffee sat in the sink. A perfect circle of green mould was floating on the surface of the liquid. Everything was on pause, waiting for my return.

I filled the bath with hot water and climbed in. My shoulders disappeared into clouds of bubbles. I leant back and closed my eyes and felt the water holding me.

When I last lay in this bath, none of this had happened. When I last slept in my bed, I didn't know Dima. When I drank the coffee in that cup, I was a different person.

I wondered if I was pregnant.

After I had climbed out of the bath, I changed the bed linen and washed up the cup in the sink. I moved things around. I wanted to change everything.

* * *

For the first couple of weeks after returning from Russia, I lived in a daydream. I refused to re-engage with London life. It didn't seem real.

I convinced myself I was carrying Dima's baby and would lie drowsily in the bath or on the sofa, lovingly touching my stomach, willing life to spring forth within me. I couldn't see beyond it. Not to be pregnant seemed incomprehensible.

But even before my period was late, I dreaded its arrival.

One evening, about a week after my return to London, I went to the theatre with a friend from Oxford.

My head was filled with Russia and Dima and the thought of a baby. During the interval, while we were sitting in the bar at the Old Vic near Waterloo station, I told her about it.

'I don't know how I will cope if I'm not pregnant,' I told her. Her eyes widened and she looked at me intently as if she were trying to decipher my meaning.

'Are you serious?'

I nodded and said I was and she laughed nervously. She asked if I was certain.

'Are you sure that's what you really want?' she said.

A woman at the table next to us was eavesdropping. I realised how insane I sounded.

I wanted to say that a miracle had occurred. I wanted to shout and scream.

But I said nothing. I lowered my voice. I told her I was certain.

'I've never felt so sure about anything,' I said.

I hovered just beneath the surface of normality. I thought that unless I was on my guard, I would be corrupted and lured back into my old life.

On the outside, I didn't look any different. I scurried to and from the office each day, but I refused to re-engage with the world around me.

I drove along the Embankment towards the *Daily Mirror* offices at Canary Wharf each morning. Before going to Russia, I had loved the drive. I could have followed the route with my eyes closed: the sweep around Parliament Square, along Whitehall, past the Cenotaph and Downing Street and Horse Guards Parade. Right on to Victoria Embankment where the London Eye stretched high in the air on the other side of the murky green Thames, curling away to the east.

Cleopatra's Needle, Waterloo Bridge, Blackfriars Bridge, Southwark Bridge, London Bridge, the Tower of London, the Esso garage on The Highway where I stopped each day to buy cigarettes and newspapers and the cashier who always greeted me like an old friend.

'Haven't seen you around for a while? Have you been away again?'

I knew where the speed cameras were, when to put my foot down to avoid fast-changing lights, rat runs back and forth across the river if the traffic was slow.

After the bright, white light of the Urals, the grey February mornings were damp and oppressive. I played the Tatu CD I had bought in Moscow on the way home from Solikamsk.

Through the car window, I watched the weary-looking commuters mechanically striding their way along the pavements, and pitied their trivial lives. They looked as if they were sleep-walking. For a few seconds, their legs moved in time to the hard metallic beat of Tatu, until they slowed down to cross a road or fumbled in a pocket for a ringing mobile phone. Behind the slightly tinted glass, they didn't seem real. Only I was awake. I had seen something different. I wasn't like that any more.

I turned up the stereo to shut them out.

Ya Soshla S Uma

I couldn't decide if I had lost my mind or if I was the only sane person around. Everyone else seemed mad to me. I wanted to shake them and tell them that none of it mattered. That there was another way to live and I had seen it.

'I don't want to be here,' I told Olga on the telephone, while I looked out of my sitting room window at the London skyline one evening.

'None of it matters any more, but I'm afraid I'll forget and my life will fall asleep again.'

A few days later, she sent me an email:

I understand your feelings so well – it always seems to me that I am back from another world and it's hard to guess which world is better.

I held on to Dima and his world by drowning my senses with anything that evoked it.

I ate cucumbers dipped in salt with little shots of vodka. I crushed feathery leaves of dill between my fingers and held them to my nose in a bid to conjure up Russia in my flat.

While I showered in the mornings before work, I would play Tatu at full volume on the stereo and transported myself back to the freezing hotel lobby in Lysva.

I wore his old Soviet dog tags hidden around my neck like a besotted schoolgirl.

When I noticed a new Russian cafe on the Fulham Road advertising 'genuine Siberian pelmeni', I parked my car on a meter and ran in to taste some.

I used copious amounts of the face cream I had used every day in Russia. Its perfume carried me back to the apartment. Even when the cream was finished, I kept the blue glass jar with its lid tightly screwed on. It held its scent like a trapped memory.

* * *

I called Dima a few days after I arrived back, hardly daring to believe that the numbers I pressed on the telephone would lead me to his voice.

Before it rang, there was a shrill tone and a click which echoed back and forth down the line, and a few seconds later I heard Dima's sleepy voice: 'Da?'

'Dima, it's Barbara,' I said. There was silence and then an astonished repetition of my name, as if he couldn't quite believe it. We began talking, struggling to make ourselves understood. Every now and then, Dima would interrupt – 'Barbara! Not quickly please! I am not English man!'

If he remembered the conversation about babies we had had on our last night together at Ivan's house, he didn't mention it – and neither did I. I was holding my breath as if exhaling would have meant breaking the spell.

So I played him his Melanie C song. I had bought the CD as soon as I arrived back in London.

'Listen Dima, listen – "I turn to you!"' When it finished we said goodbye.

'I kiss to you,' said Dima before the receiver clicked back into its holder.

*

It was clear that communication between us was going to be an elaborate and frustrating procedure. We were able to express only the most basic of emotions. Often when I telephoned, his mother Natalya answered the phone. She would try to tell me that Dima was on duty and what time to call back, and I wouldn't understand. I would call Olga and ask her to call Natalya. She would then send me an email and let me know what Natalya had been trying to tell me.

But even when Dima and I did speak, our limited vocabulary ruled out anything but the most simple of conversations. The solution, it seemed, was to write to each other – then we could express ourselves fully in our own languages and translate each other's letters with the help of a dictionary. Olga telephoned Dima to tell him about it and sent me an email the following day.

'I've just reached Dima on the telephone. Yesterday I only spoke to his mother and he was asleep.

'He told me that they don't have email at the prison, only at the post office, but Dima has never used it before and does not have any friends familiar with it. Letters take about two weeks just to travel within Moscow. It will probably take a month for a letter to reach him from England. So he'd rather go for fax connection. He promised to investigate and call in a few days.'

In the end, Dima heard of someone who had a computer with an Internet connection in Berovsk, a town neighbouring Solikamsk. He didn't know the man who owned it, but through a tenuous chain of four or five friends, he managed to get permission to use it.

He carefully read out the email address to me over the

phone and asked me to label each one I sent 'FOR DIMA' so there would be no mistaking who it was for.

He received my first and sent one back – but my computer was unable to cope with the Cyrillic script and a mess of nonsensical characters appeared on the screen. I forwarded Dima's first ever email to Olga. She translated it and sent it back:

Hi Barbara!!! This is the text.

> *Hello dear Barbara!*
> *This is a little letter for you in the Russian language.*
>
> *I was so glad to talk to you on the phone but it's already a week ago. I hope you are ok – both your health and your job.*
>
> *I've just received your letter by post. Thank you so much for sending the photograph that Olga took of us. We both came out so lovely, didn't we?*
>
> *Please tell me about your plans to come to Russia and see me.*
>
> *I want to see you and speak to you so much, in spite of our language problems. I hope you haven't given up learning Russian!*
>
> *Hello to you from Boris and Vladimir! They're waiting for you to come summer fishing.*
>
> *Looking forward to hearing from you very soon.*
> *Kiss you so many times,*
> *Dima*

* * *

The urge to find out if I really was pregnant became over-whelming. I couldn't stop thinking about it. The thought that I wasn't made me feel sick with disappointment. The thought that I was made my head spin.

Curiosity and fear. They battled with each other until I couldn't stand any more. On the way home on a Friday night, I bought a testing kit at the chemist by Westminster underground station. I walked home with it tucked in my bag. My period wasn't due for two days yet, but I felt certain that even a tiny amount of hormones would reveal itself. A few days wouldn't make any difference.

That night, I could hardly sleep. I thought about getting out of bed and opening the testing kit, but I had made a deal with myself that I would wait until the morning. For ten days I had convinced myself I was pregnant. But what were the chances of that really happening? I lay in the darkness savouring it, knowing that in a few hours, it could all be over and done with. Big Ben chimed four times. I lay my hand on my flat stomach. If I got up now I could settle it once and for all, but then I wondered what I would do with myself once I knew for certain. I closed my eyes, turned over and tried to go back to sleep.

When I opened my eyes, the bedroom was already lit up by the grey winter day. I looked at my clock. It was 9 a.m. I headed straight for the bathroom and picked up the pregnancy test. A minute later, I was staring at the two blue lines on the white indicator stick. I sat on the cold tiled bathroom floor trying to take it in.

It was a miracle. There was a baby growing inside me. My baby. I was saved. I took a shower and got dressed. I stared at myself in the mirror. I wondered if people would be able to see something different in my eyes.

The intercom buzzer sounded and I picked up the internal phone.

'Put the kettle on,' said a familiar voice.

It was Mr B.

8

I let him in. In a heartbeat, he was up the three flights of stairs and on my doorstep, big and blond and smiling. I made coffee and he tried to put his arms around me.

'What's this? Have you joined the army?' he joked, when his hands found the dog tags around my neck.

I told him I was pregnant and it wasn't his.

'Oh God,' he said and then hugged me tightly.

A few minutes later, he asked: 'What are you going to do?'

'Have a baby, of course,' I told him.

Once, after one of the many times we got back together after splitting up, he had told me that he dreaded finding out that I had found someone else. He had nightmares that once we were apart, I would meet someone and become pregnant with their child.

I had asked him if he would ever want to have a baby with me and he said: 'I don't see why not.' But he didn't hold his eyes to mine as he said it.

It never occurred to me to trick him. I had wanted to marry him and have a child with him, but I wanted him to come to me of his own free will. I wanted him to seek me out and find me and tell me: 'I can't live without you.'

He went out and bought folic acid and dropped off some of my clothes at the dry cleaners. He rented *Gladiator* from the video shop, roasted a chicken and fixed some loose wires along the skirting board in the hallway. We ate cream cakes and played Trivial Pursuit.

While it was clear to him that I had lost my mind, he blamed himself.

He tried to talk to me about it, but he couldn't reach me. I was perfectly complete. Untouchable. Cocooned from the world. It was as if every cell in my body trembled with anticipation. I thought about the life unfurling inside me, expanding with unstoppable energy even as I slept.

I was no longer afraid of anything. I felt calmer than I had ever felt before. I didn't worry about how I would manage, I only knew that somehow I would.

While Mr B spoke of practicalities, I was grappling with matters of life and death.

Two days later, ten people were killed in a train crash in North Yorkshire. I was dispatched to the scene of the accident near Selby and joined the pack of reporters and photographers swarming around the area. The wreckage lay like a jagged scar across the countryside. Snowdrops brushed against the ripped metal track. Forensic experts collected battered briefcases and mobile phones. Bereaved relatives brought flowers and laid them on the bridge above the broken line. It began to snow. Not Russian snow. Light flurries of wet snow whipped the cold, pinched faces of onlookers. The sky was grey and miserable.

From Selby I was sent to India to interview a half-Scottish half-Indian woman who had become a Bollywood star.

Mr B was angry when I called him from Heathrow airport.

'How can you even think about going away at a time like this? You need to sort things out. Tell them you can't go.'

'There's nothing to sort out,' I told him.

On board the early morning BA flight to Mumbai, I bought a portable CD player so I could play my beloved Tatu.

Four thousands miles away, I met 'Bollywood Babe' Helen Brodie at her beachside apartment. Voile drapes billowed at the open French windows. A bougainvillaea-covered balcony looked out over the glittering blue Indian Ocean. I was even further east than Dima in the Urals. Standing in the cool sea breeze, I thought how vast the world was.

The next morning, I woke up in my bedroom at the Taj Palace hotel feeling nauseous with hunger. I ordered toasted cheese sandwiches and coffee and when I'd finished those, I ordered some more. Afterwards, I realised it wasn't hunger. The nausea was still there. Morning sickness had begun.

I lay by the pool, staring up at the hot, muggy sky.

Mr B called.

'I don't think you've thought this through,' he barked down the phone. 'Have you any idea how exhausting it is raising a child? Do you know how much childcare costs? The figures just don't add up.'

I laughed rebelliously and told him I didn't care. His voice sounded far away. When he carried on ranting, I hung up, put my earphones in and listened to Tatu. I closed my eyes and my head filled with the sounds of their mournful shrieks. Nothing mattered except what was inside me. Occasionally I opened an eye to see Mr B's number flashing up on my phone. When he refused to give up, I switched it off.

He left a message. His voice was softer. He said he was sorry he had shouted, he was just worried about me. My new bed had been delivered. He had taken a photograph of it on his digital camera and emailed it to me. I switched on my laptop and saw the bed next to the window in my cool, white bedroom. Through the sash window, the branches of the plane trees on the pavement outside had begun sprouting tight buds of white blossom. I longed for home.

I arrived back in London early in the morning after a night flight into Heathrow. My father and stepmother had been staying in my flat. I told them over breakfast that they were going to be grandparents.

They took it well. Perhaps they had also despaired that I would ever meet anyone.

At least this way, even if I missed out on marriage, I wouldn't be denied having my own child because of it.

I told my mother a few days later. Her face drained of blood and an involuntary 'Oh God!' burst from her lips.

'I'm really happy about it,' I stuttered, covering my sobbing eyes with my hands.

She said: 'Well, if it's really what you want, then I'm happy for you.'

She hugged me. Practical concerns didn't matter any more. Flesh and blood surpassed all that.

* * *

A zillion miles away in Solikamsk, Dima knew nothing of my life or my treachery with Mr B.

It was hard to feel that anything I did would affect him at all. He seemed too strong, too stoical.

I couldn't imagine him being hurt or angry or shocked. I was the one thrashing around in search of the right way. Dima didn't question anything.

I looked at the photographs I had taken of him. I remembered the musty smell of his uniform and its rough canvas texture against my skin. I wondered what our baby would look like.

Olga had broken the news on the telephone that he was going to be a father for the second time.

'Oh my God,' she said, laughing, when I told her. 'It's just incredible.'

I had asked her to call Dima for me, knowing that although by using simple words I could have made him understand I was pregnant, it would be impossible to gauge his response accurately.

She called Dima and called me back immediately after their conversation.

'He wants you to telephone him,' she said. 'I told him he should sit down because I had something to tell him and he knew straight away. I think he is in shock.'

When we spoke minutes later, it was hard to know what to

say. His voice sounded far away. I closed my eyes and tried to see the face of my saviour.

'You are happy?' he asked me on the distant, crackling line.

'Yes, very happy,' I replied.

'*Ya toja*,' he said softly. 'I am happy too.'

At my first antenatal appointment, I answered the questions the midwife asked as she built up a picture of my medical history and that of my baby's father.

'Any incidents of strokes, hereditary illnesses, congenital diseases on his side of the family?' she asked brusquely, her pen poised to tick the list in front of her. She nodded patiently when I told her I'd find out.

I briefed Olga with my list of questions and she faithfully reported back.

'He says not to worry. There's no brain disease on his side of the family.'

'No there's nothing,' I told the midwife at the next appointment. 'There's nothing to worry about at all.'

I sent Dima a copy of the first hazy scan picture, taken twelve weeks into the pregnancy when the baby was just six centimetres long, a confused bundle of DNA from two different worlds, a chance encounter that would bind our ancestry together.

* * *

In the office, I hid my burgeoning waistline beneath loose-fitting tops and struggled to write about other people's lives. I delayed telling anyone I was pregnant for as long as possible.

After I finally broke the news, I got used to hearing whispering behind cupped hands. Half-truths. No one dared to ask what had happened or to show how shocked they must have been. The way my editor looked at me changed – as if I'd already moved on and was no longer useful to him. Everyone could see that I was lost to another world. I was untouchable.

I found it hard to disguise the fact that I didn't want to be there. The pettiness of it all left me numb.

Newsreader Fiona Bruce was expecting her second child: 'It's nappy news for TV Fiona!'

Two American sisters had invented a science of female sexuality: 'The Viagra Twins!'

I wrote about sex and prenuptial agreements; how the Spice Girls had matured into women: 'Famous Five Grow Up'.

I fought the urge to scream and shout and say that none of it mattered.

At home, Mr B's clothes were hanging in the wardrobe once again. I had given him a spare set of keys. We were slipping back into our old ways. Romantic breakfasts at the Savoy. Weekends away together. We flew to Spain to stay at a palazzo near Seville. It was the end of April: too cold to swim in the courtyard pool. We walked hand-in-hand in the gentle spring sunshine, ate ice cream and watched the bullfights in the Real Maestranza bullring.

Bulls' blood clotted the sand in sticky pink rivulets. I wondered if looking at it was good for the baby. I thought about Dima and our cockroach-ridden bedroom in Solikamsk, then looked at Mr B sitting next to me.

Russia hardly seemed real any more.

Love smelled of Roget et Gallet soap on warm, clean skin.

His mobile phone rang. It was a friend.

'I'm in France. Just doing a bit of work,' he lied. The matador plunged another dart into the bull's neck.

'I can't do this any more.' I told him when he'd finished the call. 'I'm having a baby. I need to be settled. We have to decide this once and for all.'

When we got home, Mr B made an appointment to see a divorce lawyer. He said things were different. He had changed.

'I can't go on living a lie,' he said. I had never heard him speak like that before.

On the day of the appointment, I kissed him goodbye and set off for the office. At lunchtime, I called to see how things had gone, but his phone was switched off.

The old sickness came back. Fear and panic and anger. I couldn't breathe. Finally I heard his voice on the end of the phone. He was at my flat. I asked him how his meeting had gone but the tight pain in my chest told me all I needed to know.

He tried to speak with casual lightness: 'The solicitor cancelled the appointment. She's off sick today.'

I told him: 'You're lying.'

He said: 'No, really.'

I screamed: 'Don't lie to me!'

His voice wavered and returned to its usual tone.

'I'm sorry, Barbara. Please don't be angry with me. I couldn't go through with it. This is really hard for me.'

I told him to take his things and get out of my flat.

I hissed at him: 'Put the keys through the letter box and never come back.'

*

I cried for a while and then I looked down at my thickening waist and stomach. I had read that an unborn baby could feel its mother's emotional turmoil. I felt guilty. I stopped.

I retreated into my own little world, a world where only the baby and I mattered. I stopped feeling alone. When I wasn't working, I spent most of my time in my bed, wrapped up in a white goosedown duvet, reading. I craved stuffed vine leaves and peas and cottage pie. Weeks passed by. My stomach began to swell. The air got warmer. The giant plane trees, thick with leaves, whispered outside my bedroom window. I slept with it open so I could hear them.

Dima sent another email.

Hello, dear Barbara,

Thank you so much for the picture of the baby. I'm very, very glad that both of you are OK. I am happy to know that our baby is big already.

Can you send a photograph of yourself? On the one you sent through the Internet, all I can see is my own face. What I cannot see here is your face, to say nothing of yourself. And I'd like to see what the house you live in looks like. Is that possible?

What about your plans? Please write to me and tell me about all your thoughts. You should write to me in English, because it is much more interesting for me to study English by reading letters from you than by reading those dull text books.

What I am really sorry to say is that my English is still so poor that I had to ask a friend of mine to help me translate this letter. I'm sure one day I will read and write English without much trouble.

When I read an English text book, I often wish I could read an article of yours instead. I am far more interested to know what you write and think about. I'd like to know you inside out (I heard those words in an English song the other day).

Barbara, you should know that I am longing to see you. I do hope we will live to see this happen one day – won't we? My mother said I should ask you to come and see us as soon as possible.

Well that's all for the day, perhaps.

Please give my best regards to your parents and lots of love to you.

Yours Dima.

I got out my credit card, called Aeroflot and booked a flight to Perm via Moscow.

9

Olga was impressed by the size of my stomach when she met me at Sheremetyevo airport. I was nearly six months pregnant and it had stretched into a perfectly taut mound.

'I think it's going to be a big baby, Barbara,' she said in amazement. 'How on earth will it ever come out?'

As soon as she had heard of my plan to return to Solikamsk, she had insisted on coming with me.

'You can't travel there on your own,' she said. 'I don't think it's safe for you.' 'Besides,' she added, 'I love our little trips together.'

We retraced our steps to the Urals, taking a night flight from Moscow to the city of Perm. In February, we had taken off during a blizzard. Now Moscow simmered. The plane soared into the steamy night. The inky sky was clear and as we travelled eastwards, the first curves of the morning sun slipped above the horizon and blotted out the stars.

Half an hour before landing, I took out a mirror from my bag and stared at the pale half-moons of tiredness beneath my eyes.

I thought of Dima in a car heading towards the airport to meet us and wondered how he pictured me. My face was rounder, my hair cut shorter. I reapplied my make-up and buried my exhaustion beneath a layer of powder and lashings of mascara. Then, I closed my eyes and tried to recall the very first time I had seen him sitting in Boris's office. I tried to remember how certain I had felt.

He was waiting next to the luggage hut on the edge of the runway. His tall, slim frame stood out in the middle of a crowd of people waiting for friends and relatives. He hadn't yet seen me.

Olga and I walked across the runway towards him. My heart was in my mouth. He suddenly turned and looked over and I couldn't raise my eyes to his. He threw away his cigarette, stepped towards me and stooped awkwardly to give me a kiss on both my flushed cheeks.

I thought how strange it was that we were here together again – as if I had stolen part of his soul and returned to the scene of my crime.

We drove towards Solikamsk in his Uncle Tolya's car. Tolya wore a clipped, stiff moustache like the one Stalin always had, and occasionally nodded and smiled in the mirror at Dima and I in the back. He and Olga chatted in the front.

Out of sight, Dima reached for my hand and brushed it with his thumb. He moved his other hand on to my stomach. It felt hot through my jersey dress.

'And how is our baby?' he whispered.

I lifted my eyes and looked up at him properly for the first time. I wondered if he could still save me.

90

*

Russia looked different. The drifts of snow that had swamped it in winter were gone. Summer sun shimmered on dusty beige concrete. Without winter's protective coating of ice on the road, the car thudded across pot-holes as we passed through hundreds of miles of pine forests.

The sharp colours of winter were muted in the hazy light. The ghostly silver birches swayed in the breeze.

One by one, the landmarks Olga and I had passed in a taxi five months earlier appeared at the roadside: the Second World War memorial statue in a forest clearing; the sharp right turn past a field filled with tiny wooden dachas; the roadside cabin selling warm cabbage pies.

With every mile that passed, London loosened its grip. Out of sight, it was hard to believe it still existed.

Warm air rushed through the open car windows and washed over us. In winter, the dry frozen air had trapped the harsh scents of Russia: diesel fumes, stale tobacco, wet gloss paint and crushed dill. In the blank summer heat they mingled with the crisp smell of grass and pine.

I breathed deeply and layers of anxiety floated away. In the back of the car, I felt Dima's leg pressed against mine and I rested my head against his shoulder.

Four hours after leaving Perm airport we reached Solikamsk. The old potassium extraction plants and abandoned salt mines on the outskirts of the town reared up to greet us as the road finally descended into the centre.

We emerged at Revolution Square. Our old hotel stood on the left. It looked as bleak and deserted as it had on the day we arrived in February.

Dima's eyes followed my gaze towards the apartment windows on the top floor. The dazzling sun reflecting off them transformed them into black squares set into the grey wall. It was impossible to see through them.

I pictured our room inside: the giant radiators, the garish threadbare carpet, the cockroaches crawling behind the peeling wallpaper. I longed to be safely back inside the lumpy bed, curled up for ever beneath the turquoise nylon bedspread with the snow falling softly against the frozen window.

* * *

Dima's home in Ulitsa Lenina was a one-bedroom apartment on the fourth floor of an ugly yellow-grey Soviet block with rusting balconies. Television aerials on the flat roof thrust into the cloudless sky like dead stalks. The year of Block N5's construction – 1974 – had been roughly painted at the top in blood-red paint by the prison convicts who had built it.

The concrete stairs leading to the fourth floor had subsided slightly. I felt giddy and lopsided as I climbed them.

The apartment door was already open. A white-haired woman with brown eyes and smooth cream skin stood waiting, her arms outstretched.

'My daughter, my daughter, my daughter.'

Dima's mother, Natalya, rocked me in her soft, warm arms while she murmured softly in Russian.

She ushered us into the tiny sunny kitchen to eat, stirred sour cream into bowls of cabbage and meat soup and then placed them in front of us. When I had finished, she filled the bowl again.

'For the baby,' she told Olga. Dima stood beside her, nodding sternly in agreement.

Afterwards, we drank sweet black tea and ate bread and honey taken from the bees kept by Dima's grandfather. Natalya gave me a necklace – a smooth oblong of lime wood on a piece of string.

'It's a talisman. To protect the baby and bring you both good health,' she said, taking my hand in hers and turning to smile at Dima.

From a radio on top of the fridge, the voice of a man was announcing the productivity results for the local collective farm. It was monotonous and soothing.

Outside, laughing children chased each other between the blocks of flats. A dog barked. A train rattled by along the railway track at the bottom of the road. I had stepped between two worlds but knew that each swirled on whether I was there to witness them or not. Waves of tiredness washed over me.

I was too exhausted to think about it any more.

The only bedroom in the flat was Dima's. We lay down on an old brown divan to sleep. It didn't open out properly and the two gently sloping sides gradually nudged us closer and closer together. He put his arms around me and fell asleep.

Next to us, an enormous poster covered the entire wall with a photograph of a wild, rocky coastline battered by a stormy sea.

A door leading from the room out into an enclosed balcony was open. A gentle breeze filtered through the midday heat. It ruffled Dima's hair.

I looked at his face. It was uncomplicated and uncorrupted.

I thought about how kind and gentle he was. How he had accepted me without question. How he had never done anything to hurt me.

I wondered how I could have doubted him. Lying next to him, I felt as sure as I had in winter. But the madness and hysteria had gone. He soothed me. The baby twitched inside me, as if it knew it was home.

10

In the garden of a country dacha belonging to Yulia's grand-mother, Boris was digging. He emerged from the middle of a vegetable patch framed by a fence hung with the rotting carcasses of dead crows. He was covered in dirt and sweat, and clutching an old copper coin.

He folded my hand around it.

'Present,' he said.

I opened my fingers and looked at the treasure inside.

It was dirty, slightly eroded and bluish in colour, as if it had been nestling in the soil for a couple of hundred years. The coin was a 'Polushka' – a quarter of a Kopek – minted in 1751, ten years into the reign of Empress Yelizaveta Petrovna, the daughter of Peter the Great.

When the dirt was washed off, the Imperial Eagle revealed itself once more, wielding its staff and sceptre defi-antly.

Beneath the turmoil of the ever-changing world above, Russia was solid and immutable.

I looked up at Boris and a smiling Yulia standing behind him. Major Tyshchenko stood up from a garden bench. He was immaculately dressed in his khaki, green and burgundy uniform. They were all there, welcoming and warm. Nothing had changed.

It was our first evening in Solikamsk. Dima had organised what he called a 'reyoonyon'.

'We never believed that you would come back. You are a very good girl,' said the Major, clapping his hands on my shoulders and kissing me on both cheeks.

My return was seen as a gesture of loyalty and friendship. They had thought it so unlikely that I would travel halfway around the world to see them, and yet there I was. The fact that I was pregnant with a Russian baby drew us even closer. It was the most romantic story they had ever heard, and they were proud to be a part of it.

Yulia's pale blonde hair had been cut short and her face was tanned. She broke off from weighing buckets of red potatoes and rubbed her soil-covered hands on her jeans. We hugged each other.

'Is the baby moving yet?' she asked excitedly. 'You must tell me, I want to feel it.'

Land that had been covered in a swathe of pure unbroken white in the winter was now swollen with life. Radishes, cucumbers, potatoes, parsley and dill, strawberries, raspberries, artichokes and cabbages had been crammed in side by side.

The domes of St Trinity Cathedral peeped up in the distance behind the orchard trees. In winter, icicles had hung like silver ropes from the Orthodox crucifix at the top. Now it glistened gold in the evening sun.

We sat around a wooden table tucked beneath the eaves of the dacha and drank beer.

Above our heads, small fish, caught by the men in the Kama river earlier in the summer and swathed in salt, had been lined up, pegged on to a makeshift washing line and left to dry in the sun.

Dima took some down, cut off their heads with the knife in his pocket, and showed me how to peel their skin and eat the chewy, salty flesh underneath.

Yulia washed radishes from the garden and cut bunches of parsley to eat with the fish.

Boris poured petrol on an old rusty barbecue which wobbled precariously on three legs. He cooked *shashlyk* – cubes of pork marinated in jars of water and onions and cooked on skewers.

When we had finished them, Yulia brought bowls of blackcurrants smothered in sugar.

She kissed my cheek.

'She says she loves the way you smell,' said Olga. 'She wants to know if you use French perfume.'

Butterflies drifted across the garden. Bees skimmed the flowerpots. Dima draped his arm across my lap. It was strong and tanned and safe. Yulia continued measuring out portions of potatoes on weathered black scales that had been used by her family for over a century. She placed them in plastic bags, ready to be collected by her ninety-five-year-old grandmother and sold in the market.

'We are the only family in Solikamsk to grow this type of

potato,' she said proudly, waving one at Olga. A tiny wizened old lady dressed in a rust-coloured jacket and a white headscarf appeared at the gate. She picked up the precious bags of potatoes while keeping her narrowed eyes fixed on me.

'Who is she?' asked Yulia's *babushka*. Yulia gave her a short explanation about the *Anglichanka* at the bottom of her garden.

'From England? Pregnant? What on earth does she want with a Russian man?' she said, rolling her eyes in despair.

After dinner, I showed them the postcards I had brought to give Katya to take into her school: Big Ben photographed from across Westminster Bridge, a red London bus, a telephone box, a black cab, the London Eye on the edge of the Thames.

The men laughed at the Coldstream Guards on parade outside Buckingham Palace.

'Are they women?' asked the Major disdainfully, when I explained to him that sometimes the weight and heat of their bearskin hats made them faint in summer.

'Katya will love them,' said Yulia.

Katya had been dispatched to pioneer camp as soon as the school term had ended, following in the footsteps of millions of Russian children since the days of Lenin.

Under Soviet rule, Olga explained, it was mandatory for youngsters to join The October Children when they turned seven. At the age of nine, when they had already learnt to be good communists, they graduated to The Young Pioneers.

For three months in the summer, the faithful little comrades would wake each morning, dress themselves in their neat white shirts and red scarves and caps, and line up outside, ready to sing the Soviet anthem and salute the flag as it was raised up the pole.

At night, they sat around campfires singing Communist anthems:

> *We'll set fire to this blue night,*
> *We're all Pioneers, children of workers . . .*

The tradition had survived, despite the collapse of Communism, but the line-ups and uniforms had been replaced with swimming, volleyball and picnics. The songs they sang had changed. They were looking to the future now.

Like Dima, Boris, Yulia and the Major before her, Katya was spending her summer twenty miles away with hundreds of other youngsters.

'Did you enjoy going there?' I asked Dima, when he and the others recounted their own pioneering experiences.

'I found it rather boring,' he conceded, 'but everybody went. It's what you did.'

'I didn't go,' said Olga. 'My mother was convinced that it was too dangerous with all those boys around.'

Olga's mother had been wise. Away from the watchful eyes of Yulia, the now twelve-year-old Katya was, in fact, exploring her new-found interest in boys, and her young face was flushed and excited when we visited her the following day.

The pathway leading into the camp cut across a lake smothered in thick fluffy white poplar seeds. Katya was charging around on long, skinny legs across a tarmac court in the middle of a game of basketball. Boris shouted at her to join us.

She blushed and squirmed when Yulia demanded to know why she had written the name 'Grigoriy' across her forearm in giant letters.

Boris waved his arms to silence her: 'Oh leave her be! She's having fun.'

We sat on a bench next to a broken, half-sunken rowing boat and a statue of Lenin and she giggled nervously while I showed her the presents I had bought from a souvenir shop next to Victoria Station – a t-shirt, a mug, a pencil case – all covered in the Union Flag. She stared down at them.

'When your baby is born, Barbara,' she asked, 'will it be Russian or English?'

Dima and I discussed the same question later.

'I want that our baby speaks Russian,' he told me, as if its linguistic persuasion depended on me alone.

'But Dima,' I said, 'the baby will only speak Russian if you are there to speak Russian to it.'

I tried to imagine Dima in London. I couldn't picture him there. It was all wrong.

'What will I do? Sweep the streets maybe?' he asked me, with a depressed look on his face.

The possibility of me going to live in Solikamsk seemed just as ridiculous to him.

In the first dreamy stages of pregnancy, I hadn't given much thought to what would happen after the baby was born. Now, I was starting to wonder what I would do. When Dima pictured London he had no comprehension of the stark reality. I couldn't afford to live there and look after our baby, and if I went back to work, we would be apart most of the time. In Russia, I reasoned, I would be able to stay at home with my baby.

I tried to explain it to Dima.

'It's not good here for a baby,' he said, highlighting the poor medical facilities, the pollution, the lack of decent food in winter, the severe climate.

'And what would you do here anyway?' he asked.

'I don't know.' I said. 'I'd be able to look after our baby. Maybe teach English, maybe just live.'

He looked at me as if I was insane.

'No Barbara,' he said, shaking his head. I asked Olga to talk to him about it later.

'He can't understand why someone from London would want to bring a baby out here,' she explained after talking to him. 'He won't even consider it.'

I thought about the satellite TV channels he watched. The wealthy West was regularly dangled in front of him. It seeped into his mind like a drug. He was haunted by the consciousness that something better existed, but paralysed by the conviction that it would for ever remain out of his reach. Nothing would make him understand why anyone else would want to give up such a life.

One evening he showed me a video he had made when he visited an old school friend from Solikamsk who had gone to eastern Germany to find work.

The first few minutes of the tape were ordinary enough. A group of Russian men sat around a small table that was covered in overflowing ashtrays. The kitchen of his friend's flat was filled with empty bottles. A woman placed salt cucumbers and vodka on the table. They cheered and raised their glasses towards Dima behind the video camera.

But as the film moved outside the following day, Dima trained the camera on the shiny BMWs in a car park, and then on the window of a mobile telephone shop.

In one scene, his friends took him to the city's car scrap heap and they stood around, shaking their heads and pointing in disbelief. Vehicles that would have drawn astonished, admiring glances in Solikamsk had been discarded and were waiting to be crushed.

Lying in bed one night, I asked Dima about the giant poster of the wild, stormy sea which overshadowed us.

'It takes me away from here,' he told me.

'You don't want to be here?' I asked him, and when he let out a cynical laugh and shook his head, I added defensively: 'I like it here very much.'

He looked around the room and then back at me. He tutted.

'No Barbara,' he told me, 'I don't think you understand the Russian life.'

'I understand. I understand,' I objected.

We stared at each other stubbornly. Neither of us would back down.

'Life in England is not so good,' I said, but it was impossible to explain why. It wasn't just a problem of language. Even so, I couldn't bear his determination to deconstruct the world I considered such a wonderful antidote to my own.

In a bid to win this battle of lifestyles, I appealed to his national pride.

'Don't you love your country?' I asked him.

He paused and threw me a look that said I was cheating.

'Yes, I love my country,' he conceded slowly with a sigh, 'But I don't like it very much.'

11

It was the height of summer and each day there were only three hours of darkness. Night was as brief as a passing shadow, and the stifling hot days stretched on interminably.

The heat left a constant film of sweat on my skin, and the night-time sun offered no respite. I would lie as still as I could on Dima's bed, watching him stand inside the enclosed wooden balcony.

Bare-chested, he would lean out of the open window and smoke a cigarette while he gazed towards the silver streaks of the Usolka river and the railway tracks and the green expanse beyond.

When it was impossible to sleep, we sat inside the balcony and played chess among pots of dusty African violets. Tucked inside this tiny haven, jutting perilously out over the street below, he would force me into checkmate in only a handful of moves. While I pondered which way to steer the wooden pieces which had been elaborately carved by one of the prisoners at Bely Lebed, his calm blue eyes gave no hint of the defeat that lay waiting for me around the corner.

I never turned down an opportunity to challenge his ruthless genius, but, to my intense frustration, I never once won a game against him.

'He has a devious mind,' said Olga when I complained at my run of bad luck.

I was deaf to her warnings that all Russian men were the same. Impending motherhood, she said, gave me more in common with the women of Solikamsk than speaking their language could have done.

We saw them walking along the streets pushing tatty, old-fashioned pushchairs handed from mother to mother. Their hard-bitten angular faces were pinched with exhaustion and disillusionment. Like the skimpily dressed teenagers in the hotel lobby in Lysva, they had once poured all their energy and ambition into ensnaring a man. Driven only by the desire to conceive and be married, they had been granted their wish. But the men who fathered their babies were nowhere to be seen.

There were no young, smiling couples taking a stroll together and taking it in turns to push their children. Most of them got married after falling pregnant, and brides with large bouquets held in front of their extended stomachs were a common sight. But as Olga so often pointed out, more often than not, such marriages ended in divorce.

All over Solikamsk, mothers and daughters were raising grandchildren alone while a generation of outcast men found companionship with each other and in vodka. They clustered round the vodka kiosks near the market, clutching bottles of beer in one hand and little glasses of spirit in the other. Their eyes were glazed over. They couldn't feel any more. They were immune to the world.

Despite Olga's ominous warnings about the future, for now Dima and I were still a couple.

He was mine in a way that Mr B had never been.

Romantic love was dangerous and painful. What Dima and I had was far more real than that. We were bound up by simple, unquestionable truths. He was the father of my baby. Our souls were entwined.

Our conversations were becoming easier, with the help of Natalya's old dark green 1950s dictionary. It offered up the strangest-sounding words when he was trying to express himself.

'You are grave?' he said when he asked if I was serious about the possibility of coming to live with him in Solikamsk.

On another occasion, he asked if I planned to feed our baby with 'the bosom'.

In turn, I grappled with his language, trying to curl my Anglo-Saxon tongue around rolling Slavic words. He opened his mouth wide to show me how to make a deep well with my tongue to resonate the Russian 'L'.

Progress was slow, but we managed quite well with our hybrid Russian-English – and when we didn't, we would shout for Olga's help.

But we were just as content to sit in silence.

The rhythm and routine of each day became reassuring and hypnotic.

Natalya, who usually slept on the sofa in the living room, spent her nights at a friend's dacha, and Olga took her place.

Each morning, I woke to the sound of her key in the door and listened to her moving around the kitchen.

The smell of fresh soup would filter into the bedroom. Natalya sliced bread and laid out the table with pickled cucumbers and mushrooms, cheese and meat before calling us to the table to eat breakfast.

She spoke Russian slowly to me, acting out her words and laughing when I didn't understand. She showed me how to salt cucumbers with dill. She made tea from lime tree leaves.

After she had finished making us breakfast, she hand-washed clothes in the tiny bathroom and pegged the dripping garments from a line above the old stained bath.

There was no hot water in the block of flats during the summer months, and daily washing was an elaborate procedure. Every morning, Dima patiently heated up double the quantities of water he usually prepared for himself and Natalya in large pans on the stove. He would carry the scalding hot containers to the bathroom, staggering perilously under the weight of them and throwing me an indulgent look that said: 'Oh, you and your pampered English ways!'

I would crouch in the bath with the wet clothes flapping around my head, and mix the boiling water with cold in a plastic bowl before washing with clumsy, splashing movements.

'When does the hot water get turned on?' I asked him one day.

'At the end of August,' he replied, 'sometimes the beginning of September; whenever the municipal water authority decides to do it.'

Even cold water couldn't be taken for granted. Dima and Natalya had filled dozens of plastic buckets with water from the taps and placed them around the flat. Some were tucked beneath the kitchen table, others on the balcony and in the bathroom – in readiness for the all too frequent days when the water supply was turned off altogether.

While I carried out my elaborate bathroom rituals, Olga would quietly dress herself and disappear to church. She carried religious icons in her make-up bag and spoke with zeal about the God she had been denied under Communism. When she returned at the end of the services, she seemed brighter and more purposeful, as if she'd been reminded of all the good things in her life.

One morning, she looked troubled.

'I would very much like to pray for you, Barbara,' she said frowning at me.

'Please feel free,' I replied, happy to accept any positive force into my life.

But even religion, it seemed, was not above the Russian obsession with rules.

'Oh no!' she replied, 'I don't think it's allowed because you are not Russian Orthodox. I'll have to ask.'

Dima and I went to buy food, and we did it the old Soviet way. In a small sickly smelling grocery shop, we queued up to pay for a loaf of dense, oily bread and then waited in another line with our receipt to collect the unwrapped loaf. We repeated the routine again at the meat counter to buy a roll of ham and then at the cheese counter. Every item on sale was out of reach or on display behind glass. Women wearing delicate pink paper hats moved efficiently behind the counters, collecting the goods we had already paid for.

We found apple juice and a jar of Nescafe Gold Blend and bright yellow Lipton tea bags. We bought long-life milk, a scoop of sugar knotted in a flimsy plastic bag, and milky, sugary Russian chocolate.

Dima pulled a scrunched-up plastic carrier bag from his pocket. They were like gold dust. If you wanted one in the shop, he explained, you had to pay, and you didn't even get a new one. An old man bent double by age was putting a grey package into one marked 'Calvin Klein'. Another woman had been given a green and white bag from the Spanish department store, El Corte Inglés.

It was hard to believe I would ever cruise the aisles at Sainsbury's again. We walked away from the shop hand-in-hand. London seemed ugly and irrelevant. When I thought about it, I felt its oppressiveness closing in on me. Winter's feelings returned. I felt free again. With Dima by my side I was invincible.

12

In 1917, just as Lenin and the Bolsheviks were about to seize power, fifty-year-old Sergiy Petrovich Ilmensky was appointed Bishop of Solikamsk by the Russian Orthodox Church.

The tendrils of Communism took time to spread out as far as the Urals, but by December 1918, the head of the Cheka, Russia's secret police, had ordered the Bishop's arrest.

The day after he was seized, he was drowned in the Kama river. Stripped of his clothes, his long hair was braided in plaits and sticks put through them by a frenzied mob. Two benches were placed either side of a large ice hole and two executioners stood on them. The Bishop was raised into the air and then lowered through the hole into the deathly cold water below.

After half a minute, he was raised and then lowered. After twenty minutes, his body was covered with a sheet of ice two inches thick – but, for a few minutes more, at least, he still lived.

'If you stand on the riverbank at night,' Dima told me, 'they say you can still hear his screams.'

*

The mighty Kama was a river of extremes: frozen and deathly and white in winter, and cool and blue in summer. Six months before, Olga and I had walked knee-deep in snow to see men and women with home-made rods dangled through ice holes, waiting for the fish below to bite. It was so white, the only way to determine where land and water met was by looking to see where the trees began growing.

Now the Kama was wide and blue, framed at the sides by emerald green rushes and yellow flowers that whispered in the wind. Its deep waters were brimming and alive with quicksilver fish. We stood on the pebbled shore. Waves rolled in at our feet.

Dima and Boris had decided that if I was to understand fully the essence of Russianness, we should undertake a little camping trip.

'Feesh, Barbara, feesh,' Boris had said, miming the action of casting a line into the water.

Love of nature coursed through the veins of Russians. It was a peculiar affair. On the one hand, Solikamsk residents clamoured for flats in the soulless grey blocks. They left the elderly to occupy the pretty wooden dachas with their elaborately painted window frames, banyas, wood-fired ovens and outside toilets.

But every weekend in the late summer, the town emptied out towards the forests and the rivers. People searched for mushrooms and berries with almost spiritual fervour.

Even devout Muscovite Olga shared in this strange behaviour. I had seen her stop in the street, her nose twitching, and watched her sniff the air like a bloodhound. She would wander off the pavement towards nearby bushes without a word, as if she had been possessed. Even when I could smell nothing, she would insist there were mushrooms nearby.

Men and women would happily sit for hours by the river, never minding that their reward would often only be a couple of tiny fish.

'The Kama is the place where my soul feels at peace,' explained Dima with surprising seriousness when I asked him about these excursions. I didn't like to ask if this rural nirvana was also aided by vodka.

Boris and Dima had planned the trip with military precision. Fidel, the inappropriately named driver who had taken a shine to Olga in February, would drive us to the river. He would return to collect us two days later. For forty-eight hours we would be voluntarily marooned with no means of communication and no way of getting home.

I asked Olga what would happen if someone had an accident and she shrugged her shoulders.

I thought about the baby, perfectly formed and floating safely inside me, and looked at Dima who nodded at me encouragingly. It seemed inappropriate to start being sensible.

After picking up Dima's friend Volodya from work at the prosecutor's office in Solikamsk, Fidel had stopped the van at the edge of the Kama. Boris stood waiting with a dilapi-dated motorboat which had been dragged up on to the sandy shore.

He laughed wickedly when he saw me looking at it. 'I stole it this morning,' he said, holding out his hand to help me on board.

*

Dima put his army jacket around my shoulders and leapt over the windscreen of the boat. He perched on the front and let his feet trail in the water. Barefoot and bare-chested, his face was relaxed and peaceful. The smooth brown skin on his back was flawless, like strong milky tea. He turned and caught me staring at him, gave me a flirtatious wink, and looked away across the river.

Ten minutes upstream, we pulled into a small inlet surrounded by little wooden dachas. Naked children were diving into the water from an old, broken pontoon. They swam towards the side of the boat as Boris switched off the engine. Dima jumped off the prow, landing with sure feet at the bottom of a grassy bank, and he tied the boat to a post.

At the top of the bank, we followed Boris through a wooden gate into the garden of a rust-coloured dacha belonging to Yulia's friend Sofya.

He had brought Yulia by boat earlier, and she and Sofya were digging for worms to use as fish bait, while an elderly grey dog, named Nancy as a puppy after former US President Reagan's wife, barked excitedly and jumped in and out of the flower beds between them.

We drank cups of sweet black tea around a shaded wooden table and the faces of the others took on a happy, dreamy mask. Even Olga's porcelain face was flushed and happy.

The faceless, regimented buildings of Solikamsk had been replaced with verdant green. Here, where the silver birches grew quickly and defiantly before the deathly cold returned to freeze them through the winter months, drabness and apathy dissolved.

I saw it most in Yulia and Boris. In Solikamsk, their

relationship revolved around Yulia's chastisement of her wayward husband and Boris's sheepish mutterings as he was reprimanded for returning home at night, stupid with vodka.

Now they touched each other with the intimacy of newly-weds. Yulia stood behind Boris and draped her arms over his shoulders. She kissed his neck.

'So I'm not such a bad husband?' he teased.

'Oh, you'll do,' she replied, scrunching up his hair in both her hands.

We set off again towards a large sandbank in the middle of the river. Dima and Volodya pulled together, dragging the boat up out of the water. While Olga, Yulia and I sat on a blanket, they rolled up their trousers and unloaded the boat: blankets, tents, bottles of beer and vodka, a steel pot with a skinned rabbit inside.

Their strong bare feet trod back and forth across the sand and through the water. They erected two canvas tents – one for Boris and Yulia, and a larger one for the rest of us.

Dima looked more at ease than I had ever seen him. He gathered old driftwood, built a fire, and cast his fishing line into the river. He propped the small rod on a wooden prong, pushed deep into the sand, and sat patiently beside it.

Each fish was placed, alive, into a large saucepan of water. They were all different shapes, colours and sizes. Even Olga didn't know their English names. One had a full set of razor-sharp teeth. Dima teasingly dangled the prehistoric-looking creature over me. Its pyramid fangs bit deep into his finger, and he laughed at the expression on my face.

When the pan was full, he crouched down at the edge of the river and began cutting off their heads and slicing their bodies open. Their guts spilled into the shallow water. Blood swirled in plumes around his feet.

When he had finished preparing dinner, he stripped down to his shorts and waded into the river as if he was walking into a cornfield and parting the sheaves with his arms.

He dropped down until the water covered his shoulders and I watched him swim.

I thought how strong and capable he was. Occasionally, he turned on his back to wave at me sitting on the sand.

He slipped out of sight through the glittering blue water and around the edge of the giant sandbank. I lay back on the blanket and looked up at the endless sky.

I thought about the spiritual peace Dima had spoken about. I felt tiny and insignificant. The gentle river breeze brushed across my face. I sighed with pleasure and closed my eyes.

When I woke up, Dima was sitting beside me with a mug of tea in his hand.

He had made fish-head stew and it was time to eat. I looked into the pan and saw several pairs of eyes staring back at me. I shook my head slowly. Yulia tutted at me.

'You must feed the baby,' she said.

Dima looked offended and I took his arm.

'It's good Russian food,' he said indignantly.

I told him: 'I'm sorry,' But I wasn't sorry enough to actually eat the gruesome stew. The others devoured it hungrily, and the men washed it down with beer and vodka.

The smell of the fish made me nauseous. I sat aside from the others. I felt a scratch on one of my bare feet and I looked down.

My ankles were covered in enormous mosquitoes. As I brushed one away, another descended until my feet were speckled with black. I ran into the river to wash them off and hurriedly put on my boots. I pulled my socks up over the bottoms of my trousers and put a shirt on over my t-shirt.

'Drink vodka,' said Volodya unhelpfully. 'It keeps them away.'

But I noticed that nobody else was being bothered by them.

'It's your foreign blood,' laughed Olga.

I felt something pricking my arm and saw an engorged mosquito feeding on me through the fabric of my shirt. Its crushed body left a bloodstain on my sleeve.

By the time the men had finished their second bottle of vodka, itchy red lumps began appearing on my arms and legs. I moved beside the fire where the thick woodsmoke stung my eyes, but kept the monstrous insects away.

Having fought off nature's first attack, the second wave quickly followed. At around 10 o'clock in the evening, when the Urals sun had still not set, the sky began to turn dark. It looked odd, yellow and bruised. The harsh, squealing sound of the wind came from nowhere. It whipped the river into hard choppy waves and sent the reeds horizontal. Within minutes, the sky had turned black and sheet rain slid across the river towards our sandbank.

Inside the tent, where we ran for shelter, the canvas slapped backwards and forwards. Dima lay down and pulled a rough brown blanket over both of us. There was nothing else to do but sleep and wait for the storm to pass over.

Heavy rain pounded against the sides of the tent. Dima put

his arms around me and pulled me close to him. Out of the corner of my eye, I could see a drunken Volodya feebly pawing at Olga. He tucked a blanket around her tiny frame as she curled up on the floor, and his wandering hands reached up to stroke her hair. She snapped at him under her breath, flicked her long plait over her shoulder and turned her back on him. He sighed in resignation, lay back and closed his eyes.

It was impossible to sleep. My back ached painfully on the hard uneven floor. The blanket scratched against my skin. I stared at the damp brown canvas above, remembering in a wave of despondency that Fidel would not be collecting us for two days. I heard the whine of a mosquito, and then another. Dima snored drunkenly.

I grabbed him by the shoulders and shook him.

'Wake up! Dima,' I told him. 'Wake up.'

Nothing I could do would rouse him from his stupor. An hour crawled by. The air in the tent was hot and thick with alcohol and sweat and dampness. I couldn't breathe.

I looked across at Dima. His face was flushed and limp.

I closed my eyes and let Mr B's face appear in my mind. I looked back at myself with him in the comfort of all the luxury hotel rooms we had ever stayed in.

Once, we had driven into Paris on a hot June day in the late afternoon. The hotel, near the Arc de Triomphe, was old-fashioned and elegant. It had a creaking cage lift and original Monet paintings in the dining room. In our room, I filled the deep, deep bath and climbed in. It started to thunder and Mr B opened the balcony doors so I could smell the hot rain. We were starving. A waiter brought in a table laid out with Earl Grey tea, fresh bread, warm, ripe camembert, pomegranates and grapes. After my bath, I put on a robe and went out on to the balcony to smoke a cigarette. I leant over the stone balustrade and looked down at the people walking along the damp, steamy pavements below. I was in love. My soul soared above them.

I wondered what Mr B would have thought if he could have seen me lying there in the tent – pregnant, covered in mosquito bites, miles from anywhere.

The baby stretched and squirmed inside me. I tried to turn on to my side. The itchy blanket scratched against my skin. I saw a mosquito land on Dima's face and slapped his cheek hard. He didn't move. I swore at him before getting up, unzipping the tent door and walking outside.

It was quiet. The storm had died and the air felt clean and damp. The mosquitoes had gone. I relit the fire with some of the driftwood we had saved from the rain. I put on Dima's army jacket and lay down next to it.

Dima was hungover and dazed when he finally staggered from the tent in the morning. Yulia had screeched at him to get up.

'Please Dima,' I pleaded, 'I want to go home'. He put his arm around me, but said nothing. In the bright morning sunlight, he somehow didn't look quite so saviour-like. He looked pale and sickly. His eyes were bloodshot. His body was stiff.

An hour later, we were back on our boat, motoring down the river. I sat at the back and watched with relief as the sandbank of horrors got smaller and smaller.

We returned to the inlet and to Sofya's dacha. I went straight to the banya at the bottom of the garden. I undressed, tiptoeing around the insects crawling over the floor of the hot clammy dressing room, and opened the door to the banya itself. Inside, I washed away the clinging smell of smoke on my skin and hair.

When I came back, Yulia had made up a bed for me next to the stone oven. I climbed into it and she pulled the soft faded quilt up to my chin. I was desperate to sleep. She sat on the bed and stroked my hair, talking softly to me like a child. Her voice was like a lullaby. I looked up at her kind, gentle face and her brilliant blue eyes. They were the same colour as the water in the Kama river. It was the last thing I thought before I fell asleep.

When I woke later that afternoon, there was no sign of Dima, Boris or Volodya. They had gone off in search of more vodka.

'Once they start, they can go on for days,' said Yulia, looking at me with pity in her eyes. Her friend Sofya nodded her head in agreement. They were unable to understand why I had embarked on a relationship with a Russian man when most Russian women dreamed of meeting a Western man. But they seemed to admire my courage.

It was as if I had undertaken an endurance test and they were waiting for my face to show signs of defeat. But my choice, as nonsensical as it seemed to them, gave us a bond.

The lot of Russian women was certainly unenviable. While the men so often turned to drink to blot out the harshness of their lives, it was impossible for the women to do anything else but struggle on.

'When you are a mother, you can do nothing else,' said Yulia. 'And you can't depend on your husband for anything.'

I thought of Dima's mother setting off each day for the pharmacy where she worked, sitting behind a desk all day, checking prescriptions and ordering up supplies. She stopped at the market to buy food before returning home, where she took off her coat and replaced it with shiny overalls. She would head straight to the kitchen and begin preparing food. While we ate, she would go to the bathroom and begin washing clothes by hand. I could hardly remember ever seeing her sit down.

The only true day of rest for any of them was on the 8th of March – a national holiday they called International Women's Day. I hadn't heard of it until Dima and Olga had telephoned to congratulate me when it fell. But even then, it had never occurred to me that it was a serious celebration. In fact, it was the only day of the year that Natalya and Olga and Yulia stayed in bed in the morning while the men went out, supposedly to buy flowers for them.

In the corner of Sofya's sitting room, an ancient brown Japanese television was showing a black and white Soviet film. Female peasant farmers were thatching the roofs of their cottages. Beneath the scarves that covered their heads, they wore the hardened faces of the women on the old Bolshevik propaganda posters I had seen in my school history books.

There was no trace of femininity, no silky tresses escaped from the cloth tied tightly over their hair. Their faces were hard and weathered. They wore every wrinkle and every frown line, displayed every calloused hand with pride, like badges of honour that attested to their sacrifice and suffering.

'The Motherland calls!' One of the women let out a brief but terrified scream as she fell from the roof of one of the houses, dying as she hit the floor below. The other women hastily climbed down their ladders and gathered around her moment-arily, clucking and shaking their heads, before carrying her body away. The work continued, this time to the sounds of a rousing nationalistic song. In the grand scheme of things, one death was insignificant. The individual counted for nothing.

By the time the film had finished, the sun had slipped low in the sky. Sofya made sugary tea and we moved into the garden and waited for the men to return.

A woman in a faded cotton dress walked past the fence holding a baby in her arms. It was Rita Butorskaya, the pregnant woman I had visited in February. We were in Belkino. Without its snow blanket it was almost impossible to believe we were back in the same place. We both smiled in recognition as our eyes met and she lifted up Lilya, the daughter she had wanted so much. Rita reached out her hand towards my rounded stomach and congratulated me on the future birth of my own baby.

* * *

Natalya brought iodine from the pharmacist where she worked to tend my swollen, savaged feet the following morning.

She chastised Dima. 'You stupid boy,' she said, while she knelt down and gently dabbed the bites. 'What were you thinking of taking her out there?' He shrugged in response and walked out of the front door, shouting over his shoulder that he was going to the prison to find a driver to take us back to Perm in two days' time.

Natalya shooed me into the living room and gently pushed

me towards the sofa. She placed my feet on a cushion and covered me with a blanket while she muttered to Olga about her 'very bad boy'.

'Of course, he wasn't always so bad,' she went on, pulling an old grey photograph album from the bookshelf. She opened it up and revealed Dima's past, spread out over the cardboard pages.

He was born in Solikamsk in October 1972, four months after my own mother gave birth to me at Southampton General Hospital. He was a chubby, healthy looking baby, although Natalya told us he was a sickly child and spent the first few months of his life in hospital.

'All Russian babies are sickly,' whispered Olga, rolling her eyes.

Another photograph showed a blond-haired boy in a blue checked shirt. His eyes twinkled and his smile was angelic. The dimples were already there. There was a six-year-old Dima in a white rabbit costume, standing in front of a giant fir tree decorated with baubles and tinsel for the New Year celebrations. His hands were drawn up in front of him like paws.

Natalya smiled nostalgically at her young son.

'But oh,' she added, 'he is so like his father! He was always away serving in the army. When he was home he was never here, and it's so hard raising a son on your own.'

I turned the pages of the album slowly, trying to take in and memorise every detail, every expression. Natalya, now a fifty-year-old woman with grey hair and laughter lines, revealed her former self: a stunning, dark-eyed beauty with a chic chestnut brown bob. Dressed in a dark suit and striped tie, Dima's father, Sasha, stood at her side, his arm encircling her slim waist. The young couple stared at the camera, with shy smiles on their lips. As a family, they had been captured together standing in the snow outside the bus station in Solikamsk. While dozens of people queued behind them, nine-year-old Dima stood in front of his parents, grinning at the camera, a toy gun in one hand, wearing a fur hat that was far too big for his childish head.

A sepia shot showed Dima at eighteen following in the footsteps of his father and grandfather on his first day in the Red Army. The faded photograph looked as if it had been taken at the time of the Revolution. Dressed in his uniform and cap, he was resting his hand jauntily on the belt around his waist.

I saw him with his arm around the shoulder of his first wife Tanya, a serious-looking, pretty, dark-haired girl, and laughing as he lay on a sofa, urging his baby daughter Yulia to look at the camera. I stared at her for a long time, looking for my unborn baby's face within hers. I thought how strange it was, that while I had never set eyes on this pretty auburn-haired child thousands of miles away in Siberia, she was already the half-sister of the baby inside me.

Dima eventually returned home six hours later, smelling of beer and cigarettes and sporting a white, bloodied bandage on his right hand. He was drunk, and despite the length of his absence he had failed in his mission to find a car.

'What happened to you?' asked Olga.

He embarked on a lengthy and detailed explanation. Occasionally Olga interrupted with questions.

My patience ran out.

'What's he saying? What's he saying?' I pestered her.

She translated.

Apparently, while he was waiting for a bus to take him to the prison, a man drinking beer had knocked a bottle against him, cutting his finger.

'He expects me to believe that?' I asked Olga. I threw Dima a thunderous look.

'Oh Barbara!' she said gleefully, clapping her hands. 'Now you understand the life of a Russian woman!'

* * *

In the end, it was Dima's friend Volodya who drove us the five hours to Perm in his beloved white Lada.

He collected us from Yulia's grandmother's dacha. Boris had organised a farewell party. He, the Major and Dima had toasted the baby's health with vodka before we set off for the night flight to Moscow.

Yulia gave me some last-minute words of advice.

'The first baby is much easier than the second,' she said encouragingly. 'Because with the second you already know just how painful it is.'

'Absolutely,' agreed Dima.

When November came, he would travel to Moscow and stay in Olga's apartment while the British Embassy processed his visa application. As soon as the baby arrived, he would fly to London to see us.

'I will need a map,' he said.

I asked him what for.

He said: 'How will I find you without one?'

At the airport, he carried my bags as far as he could go without a ticket of his own. He smelt of stale beer and sweat. I felt the same sense of panic rising in my chest as I had on Valentine's Day morning at Ivan's house. After we had kissed goodbye I looked back to see him standing at the departure gate, and returned to hug him once more.

London loomed ahead of me, dark and dizzy and spiralling. I turned around and walked out of Dima's world.

13

Hi Dima,

How are you?!!!
I am lying on my sofa at home. The baby is kicking all over the place, so I think it knows I am writing to you.

When I got back on Monday, I slept for 18 hours. I have just finished work and I feel very tired. I have got my feet up, but all I can see is mosquito bites. They are much better, but sometimes they still drive me crazy itching. I think I got more bites at Perm airport. Why are Russian mosquitoes so much bigger than English mosquitoes?

I am so excited about our baby. I can't wait to see him or her! I wonder if it will look like you or me or both of us.

I cannot believe that I can get any bigger than I am now. I feel huge already.

I am aware that you did not plan this baby, I planned it. Because of that, I feel it is my responsibility. Knowing that you are happy about the baby is a joy to me and I love you for it.

Anyway, write soon. I miss you very much. November seems so far away.
   I am so impatient Dima. You are so calm compared to me.

Summer dragged on. The baby wasn't due until the beginning of November. Each day I looked impatiently for signs of autumn. I wanted to feel the first chill notes in the air.

My mind raced ahead but I couldn't see further than 'when the baby comes'. Afterwards was a golden, hazy place where I basked in the glow of motherhood. I never questioned the future. Sometimes I saw myself and my baby living in a cottage by the sea. Sometimes we were sitting among the dusty African violets in the enclosed wooden balcony at Dima's flat. Wherever I pictured us, the baby was always in my arms.

It didn't really matter where we were – as long as we were together.

It became harder and harder to get up in the mornings. I wanted to sleep and dream and shut out everything else. When the alarm went off, I would stretch out my arm and reset it with half-opened eyes. I arrived at the office later and later, and even when I got there I was barely aware of what I was writing.

Denise Lewis and Posh Spice published their autobiographies; the Prime Minister's wife was fitted with an acupuncture earring; and Al-Qaeda launched its attacks on the World Trade Center in New York. In the middle of the afternoon on 11 September, a series of gasps echoed across the

Mirror newsroom on the twenty-second floor at Canary Wharf. Journalists were crowding around the giant television screen by the editor's office. When the second plane crashed into the World Trade Center, the gasps turned to strange wails.

In my dreams that night, death pursued me. Men with guns stood waiting in the middle of the road on the way home from the office. They wanted me. I managed to escape them and drove home at breakneck speed. I ran inside my block of flats but they were waiting on the stairs.

I woke up and thought how frightening and wicked and corrupt the world was.

Dima called.

He told me that his divorce from Boris's sister Larissa had been finalised. I had asked him to do it. I didn't care that he and I weren't married, but I didn't want my baby to be born to a father who was married to another woman. It didn't matter that it was a marriage of convenience. It made me think of Mr B.

Dima had agreed, and it had been just as easy to divorce Larissa as it had been to marry her. They met back at the town hall and signed some papers in front of the ZAGS official. Larissa was more than happy to go through with it. Boris had told her about Dima and the pregnant *Anglichanka*. Larissa had already been given a small flat by the municipal property committee. She and Dima signed the forms, shook hands and walked out into the street.

He was about to set off on a weekend expedition to the forest with some friends. I heard their voices in the background. They were laughing and joking and carefree.

I pictured them together: drinking beer and peeling the

scaly skin off their salt fish, chewing the translucent pink flesh and tossing away the spines. They would sit around a fire among the birch trees. The Urals summer was over. The air would have turned cold by now. Natalya and Yulia would have already salted jars of mushrooms and cucumbers. There might still be blackberries left to pick.

Such thoughts made my heart race. Adrenaline rushed through me. I wanted to pack my bags and go straight to him.

I wanted to find him and tell him: 'Nowhere is safe if it's not with you. Let me stay here with our baby.'

But there were still nearly two months left until the birth and until then I was on my own. At my weekly antenatal classes, I looked around the room at the other expectant mothers and reassured myself that I wouldn't have wanted one of their gentle, eager husbands anyway.

I congratulated myself on my no-nonsense attitude.

If I had the baby in Russia, I would give birth alone anyway. Olga had painted a detailed picture of Russian maternity hospitals. My feet would have been strung up in stirrups while a stern-faced woman shouted incomprehensible instructions at me. Dima would have stood outside the hospital with the other fathers-to-be, swigging from a bottle of beer and waiting for news.

'Russian men are never present at the birth,' said Olga, when I told her that in Britain it was normal. 'Oh no. It's a ridiculous idea!' she replied. 'In Russia, they don't even let them inside the maternity hospital.'

Our group went on a tour of Chelsea and Westminster Hospital. In the maternity ward, the husbands looked awkward and uneasy, as if they were trespassing. Their wives clutched at their hands and looked at them lovingly.

For a fleeting moment, I wondered what it would have been like if Mr B had been there with me, holding my hand, asking questions.

I brushed the image away.

* * *

I was eight months pregnant and it felt as if time had ground to a halt.

Dima and I spoke on the phone each week. Our conversations usually followed a similar pattern. He would ask: 'How is your big stomach?' and with monotonous predictability I would tell him: 'Very, very big'. He would answer: 'I am glad.'

Once, I told him that I had been out shopping for clothes for the baby. He was furious. 'It's very bad luck,' he said. 'You must never buy clothes until after the birth.'

When he realised he had upset me, he toned down his superstitious story. 'Don't worry, my sweet. Maybe it's not bad luck in England, only Russia,' he said.

Similarly, he refused to discuss names before the big day. When I raised the subject once, he quickly silenced me. 'After the baby comes, Barbara, please. Finish talking now.'

The baby grew so large it became painful to walk. My pelvis ached dully with the weight of it. I had never felt so weary in my life.

Some friends helped me to paint the bedroom in the flat. To escape the fumes, I slept on the living room floor. Once I'd laid my heavy, awkward body down on the mattress, it took all my energy and willpower to get up again.

The telephone rang in the darkness and I rolled on to my knees and tried to push up with my hands. The telephone stopped ringing and I groaned with frustration and exhaustion.

It rang again.

I crawled across the floor and stretched out my hand to pick it up.

It was Mr B.

'Your baby must be due soon,' he said. 'I want to help you if you'll let me.'

His voice was soft and comforting and confusing. It reached out in the darkness. I closed my eyes and felt hot tears bubbling up beneath the lids.

I screamed at him.

He said he was sorry, that he had only wanted to help.

I sobbed: 'Just leave me alone.'

I went to Mothercare with a list and bought everything I needed. A neighbour saw me struggling up the stairs with a crib. 'You shouldn't be lifting that, love,' he said, and he carried it for me.

In the corner of the sitting room, a Moses basket and a blanket sat waiting for the baby's arrival. I bought a toy giraffe that played a lullaby when its tail was pulled.

After work each day, I lay on the sofa for so long that my heavy, round body left a hollow imprint when I stood up. It was the end of October and still ridiculously warm. I wore summer dresses and left my legs bare. The brittle leaves on the plane trees outside rustled and chattered.

I worked on my last story: an article about Jade Jagger. 'She's got no inhibitions. She enjoys sex and when she feels like it, she does it. Simple as that.'

Two weeks later, my waters broke.

14

It was midnight. The Embankment was almost deserted as I drove along the Thames towards Chelsea and Westminster Hospital. The dark silhouette of Battersea Power Station stretched up into the orange glow of the city night. The arching lights of Albert Bridge glittered in the choppy water. Everything looked the same. Everything was about to change.

'It's not coming yet,' said the midwife. She had connected me up to the monitor in the labour ward and was staring at the screen. 'I want to see your face contorted in agony.'

I drove home at 2 a.m. and tried to sleep.

I thought of the shiny turquoise bed in the hotel in Solikamsk and remembered the sensation of Dima's weight on me. I pictured our DNA meeting, converging, kick-starting the new life that was about to burst out into the world. I thought about the terrible night on the sandbank in the middle of the Kama river and how, even then, the baby had made its presence felt, like a beating heart inside me.

Fate had married us with a miracle.

*

There were still no contractions, but as I drifted off I could feel my stomach beginning to tighten into cramps.

My past stretched out behind me. I searched back as far as I could go, rifling through thousands of childhood memories. I saw a chubby, freckled, self-conscious child with brown-rimmed National Health specs and the chocolate brown walls of my bedroom in our little semi-detached house on a modern estate near Southampton. Images of a thousand yesterdays came thick and fast, flickering and flashing in my head: summer evenings on Daddy's little blue boat, pottering down the River Hamble, my brother and I sitting on the front singing 'Heart of Oak' until we were hoarse:

We'll fight and we'll conquer again and again!

I could still hear the echoes our voices made when we went under the bridges, and my screams when my fishing net fell off its bamboo stick and sank out of sight in the opaque green water. The blue and red swing in our garden, our pink wigwam tent. Filling up the yellow paddling pool with the hose pipe. Running into the house with grass sticking to my wet body. The playground at my primary school. The tree with the twisted trunk in the corner of the field where the tallest girl in the class, Lisa Chapman, showed us how grown-ups kissed.

It was hard to believe that the forever anxious, talkative little girl watching her was me.

I wondered how that child had got from there to here: to this moment.

*

I woke up at half past four. The cramps in my stomach felt uncomfortable, but nothing like the pain I knew should be coming. I got out of bed and made a cup of tea.

I was too excited to sleep. I tried to call Dima in Solikamsk where it was already half past nine in the morning, but the phone rang out unanswered. He had already set out through the dark snowy streets to catch the bus to the prison, unaware that his second child was about to make its entrance into the world.

In fact, the baby didn't arrive for another two days. She was finally delivered by Caesarean to the sounds of Brahms' Piano Concerto No. 2 in B flat.

* * *

I heard her before I saw her – a strange muffled cry before they had even pulled her out.

The midwife brought her to me. Her face was red and screwed up. Even while she screamed, her eyes squinted sideways towards me with a look of curiosity. I stared at her and looped my finger around her hand. Her damp dark curls were matted together with my blood.

When I held her to my breast for the first time, I thought about the hotel lobby in Lysva and the girls dressed like prostitutes, desperate to find a husband. Tatu wailed in my head.

Eventually she fell asleep in her Perspex hospital cot. She took little shallow breaths. I was exhausted but I couldn't take my eyes off her. I sat on the edge of the hospital bed and stared and stared. I searched for traits of both Dima and I. I compared my hands to hers.

When she woke she began screaming again. She cried until the centre of her forehead turned an alarming shade of purple. I walked her backwards and forwards through the hospital corridors, rocking her in my arms and whispering softly in her ear.

She looked so much like Dima it was comical. Even her hair, after I washed it, swept itself into the same style as his. It was so dark it was almost black. Her eyes were blue, and her toes and legs were long. She was his miniature.

I called Dima. I imagined him sitting at the desk in his bedroom, holding the telephone to his ear while Natalya hovered excitedly behind him. The line was engaged.

I called Olga.

'Barbara!' she squealed. 'I am talking to Dima on the other phone. He's frantic because he hasn't heard from you.'

During the three-way conversation that followed, Olga translated for both of us.

'Another girl! He can't believe it. He asks after the health of you both. Is everything ok with the baby? What about the name?'

'Anya Natalya Joan Dmitrievna,' I repeated to the registrar at Chelsea and Westminster Registry Office a couple of weeks later.

Anya had been my favourite girl's name since my grandmother bought me a book by the romantic novelist Anya Seton when I was thirteen.

It was called *Katherine*. I read into the night with a torch under the blanket until I finished it. I couldn't bear to tear myself away from the perfect, romantic past where the heroine endured a tortuous love affair and finally triumphed.

Natalya was for Dima's mother and Joan was for mine.

The space for 'father' was left blank. Without him being there to sign the register, I couldn't put Dima's name on her birth certificate. The Russian patronymic, Dmitrievna – daughter of Dmitry – was the only way of including him in her name.

He saw the first photograph of his daughter thanks to the same friend who had let him use his computer to send emails.

An image of Anya propped up in my arms appeared miraculously in colour on the computer screen in front of him.

'She looks like me,' he said proudly to Boris, who was standing next to him on this momentous occasion.

'I don't know,' said Boris, winking at him devilishly. 'I think she rather looks like me.'

15

When I looked at her I thought of miracles.

> *I am in love with our daughter, Dima. I look at her every day and thank God for her. We are so lucky to have such a beautiful, strong, daughter. I am sure she will do wonderful things with her life.*

I was a mother. For the first four months of Anya's life, we were constantly together. At night she slept by my side, waking occasionally and wailing before I kissed and fed and soothed her to sleep.

Hours blurred into days. I watched her soft pink lips clamped around my breast and felt as if we were melted together. I felt love but I also felt fear. It was as if I had been given a precious gift but knew how easily this gift might be taken away. It was hard to believe she was really mine. I was in awe of her.

At night I listened for her shallow, whispering breaths and

watched her smooth, unworried face relaxed in sleep against the pillows. I stroked her warm rosy thighs and arms and entwined her soft baby curls around my fingers.

When I slept, I inhabited a strange twilight world where the slightest whimper from Anya woke me. I dreamed she was with Dima and I inside the turquoise bedroom. Snow coated the windows. Inside, the three of us lay in the bed, safe from the cold.

During the day she cried accusingly if I tried to put her down. She couldn't bear to be still. Even if I sat down with her on my lap she would yell in frustration. I didn't mind. I carried her everywhere with me. She fitted perfectly into my folded arms. She pressed her little head between my head and shoulder. I felt her silky hair against my neck. I loved to rub my nose and lips against her temples where her creamy skin met the edge of her hair. I had never smelt anything so wonderful before.

The only time she was happy not to be in my arms was when I took her out in her buggy. I would wrap her up warmly against the heavy grey November cold and pace the streets for hours on end. The sound of raindrops falling on the plastic rain cover soothed her. The motion would finally make her sleep. I'd wander around the Tate and look at Blake and Turner. Everything was clear and pure and true. Time lost its meaning. Our days were our own.

Everyone said how beautiful she was. I smiled involuntarily when they said it but I didn't need to be told. I looked at her and could hardly believe that something so perfect had grown inside me.

Sometimes I took her to my local cafe, where the Polish

owner would break off from making bread in the kitchen for a cuddle with 'the beautiful baby'.

'Such a wonderful girl,' he would say, lifting her up above his head and rubbing his nose against hers.

I took dozens of photographs of her. While she slept. When she cried. Anya propped up on the pillows on my bed. Out in her buggy or yawning in her car seat. I sealed copies of them in an envelope and sent them to Russia.

Sometimes we walked to the King's Road to shop. Our route along Pimlico Road took us past an expensive Russian antique shop. The name of the Russian owner was written in gold above the shop door. Two early nineteenth-century ornate wooden armchairs had been placed in the window. I never went inside, even when it was raining. There was no way on earth I could afford to buy them. But I always wanted to look at the smooth mahogany arms and carved Imperial eagles. It was as if they were sharing secrets. I didn't see their meaningless price tags. I stared at them and saw history.

I didn't worry about the future. For now I was free. With Anya in my arms, I was perfectly content.

I was a mother and I thought about my own mother. There was a photograph in a baby album of me. My father took it when I was twenty minutes old. I was angry and wrinkled with a full head of dark, red curls. I had looked at the picture and seen the look on my mother's face. I knew she loved me before I was old enough to understand that look. I wished I could remember that precious, simple moment before her love for me became shrouded in guilt.

When I was seven, she moved to a Georgian cottage next to the sea. I used to sleep alone in the attic during weekend visits with my brother and stepbrother and sister. The darkness was hot, thick and dusty. I was afraid of what lay in the black spaces where the timber rafters sloped to the floor. I would lie as still as I could and listen for proof. I thought the sound of my pounding heart was footsteps coming up the attic stairs. My fear burst out from my throat.

When I called out for her – 'Mummy! Mummy! Mummy!' – she would come. She would take me by the hand and show me the black spaces in every shadowy corner. There was nothing to be afraid of.

In the middle of the night, while everyone else slept, we were alone together. For a few minutes, she was mine. When she lay my head on her chest and soothed me with words, I heard her heart beating. The skin along her breastbone was warm and oily. I felt her voice come trembling through my cheeks.

Sometimes, when I least expected it, the urge to call Mr B would creep up on me. On the way home from a walk, I would find myself looking for his glossy black car or the letters and numbers of his registration plate. My mind would take off on its own flight of fantasy. His car parked outside my flat. Mr B waiting for me to return. Mr B stepping out of the car as I arrive at my front door.

Barbara. Forgive me. I was wrong. I can't live without you.

On other occasions his voice would come back to me: telling stories.

A few days after his first child was born, his wife went out on her own for the first time since the birth and left their baby daughter with him. He decided to take a nap and laid the baby in the bed beside him. He was woken by the sound of the doorbell ringing. Mr B leapt out of bed, charged downstairs and opened the door to a friend. He invited him in and put the kettle on. They drank coffee and chatted. Only when the friend asked when the baby was due did he remember his tiny daughter with a gasp of terror. He ran back upstairs and could see no sign of her. He pulled back the duvet and found her fast asleep underneath.

We had laughed so much when he finished telling me.

They were fleeting moments that made me catch my breath. I imagined holding his hand and smiling and saying to him: 'None of it matters any more. I'm happy now.'

I didn't want him, but my happiness made me want to forgive him. But I didn't call. I brushed such thoughts away.

Precious days and weeks slipped by. I refused to contemplate the decisions that lay ahead. I had expected my old life to be swept away. But once my maternity money ran out, I knew reality would kick back in all its brutality. The thought of having to leave Anya and go back to work made my heart sick. I couldn't think about such things. They didn't make any sense. I wondered what I should do next.

I was waiting. But still Dima didn't come to find us.

16

It was New Year's Eve. Anya was two months old. While she slept beside me, the bitter wind carried Big Ben's midnight chimes into the bedroom. When I placed the palm of my hand against one of the panes of the large sash window next to the bed, I felt the cold pressing in from outside. I thought of Solikamsk, buried in snow. The old longings came back – the urge to go to Dima. I listened to the chimes. London made me feel exhausted. Russia made me think of salvation. I wanted to escape. I wanted to live a different life.

I called him and Natalya answered the phone.

'Dima, nyet! Hospital!' she said slowly and dramatically. We grappled with our dictionaries as she attempted to explain what had happened. It was clear from her tone that he was going to live and would survive his ordeal, but I hadn't a clue what she was talking about. In desperation, I called Olga and asked her to find out what had happened. She called back.

He had been involved in a drunken brawl one night and after flooring his rival, thought the matter was at an end.

But his red-faced opponent plotted his revenge carefully, lying in wait with a group of friends when Dima left the bar where he had been drinking. In the onslaught that followed, Dima's nose and cheekbone were broken and he was knocked unconscious.

'God knows how bad his injuries are,' said Olga cheerfully as she reached the end of the story. 'He's already been in hospital a week!'

Olga had once told me about Russian hospitals. I remembered her story. When she was six years old, she spent three months in one in Moscow. She couldn't remember feeling ill, only the loneliness of being abandoned in a ward filled with children aged from three months to fifteen years.

Most of all, she remembered the constant crying of the baby in the room.

'She was from the orphanage and had pneumonia,' she recalled. 'The nurse only checked on us twice a day, so the baby was always crying in her wet bed, day and night. It made us insane. She stopped crying only when she died. God forgive me, but it was such a relief.'

I looked at Anya lying asleep on the sofa next to me and at the flawless face that was so like Dima's.

In my mind, I pictured Dima lying in a sparse Russian hospital, his beautiful face battered and scarred. I imagined him being tended by stern-faced matrons in drab uniforms.

It was another week before he was sent home with a broken nose, a sore head and a bruised ego.

'I was not drinking!' he protested when we spoke on the phone.

According to his version of events, he had stepped in to defend a young woman who was being pursued by a drunken man. Dima told the man to leave her alone. When the man ignored him, Dima delivered a swift punch to his nose and sent him to the floor. So, he concluded, the moral high ground was his.

'I am to be right,' he insisted in terrible English that I didn't bother to correct.

When I finally put the phone down, I had said nothing of what really mattered. Anya and I were on our own. It was obvious that I'd have to cope without him.

I found a childminder. She was a warm, smiling woman with strong, capable hands. She lived just around the corner from my flat and after speaking briefly on the phone, I went to her house with a list of sensible-sounding questions I'd copied from a booklet.

She made me a cup of tea and then reached out for Anya.

'Let me take her for you,' she said.

While I worked my way through the list on my lap, she rocked Anya in her arms. When I reached the end and looked up, she was smiling at me. Anya was fast asleep.

I went back to work. While I sat at my desk, hammering away at the keyboard, my full, milky breasts ached in protest.

I wrote about the smallest book in the world and a girl who ran off to join a circus. The Queen Mother died and I was sent to Windsor to watch her coffin disappear through the ancient wooden gates of Horseshoe Cloister Arch at the Castle. I interviewed a teenager from Burnley who had joined – and left – the Taliban, and spent the day at the Royal Hospital for Neuro-disability in Putney with an eighteen-year-old girl, left brain-dead after overdosing on heroine in a toilet in Hastings. Her devastated mother propped her up in bed and told me: 'I know she can hear me.'

A Russian passenger jet en route to Spain collided with a DHL cargo plane above the Swiss–German border, killing forty-five schoolchildren from Ufa in central Russia.

Life was as tragic and fragile and shocking as ever.

Each day, I wrote as fast as I could and then hurried home to collect Anya and bath her and feed her before bedtime.

Winter softened into spring. My milk dried up. The evenings got lighter. When I picked Anya up, there was still time to take her to St James's Park. We fed the ducks and sat on the grass and watched the squirrels weaving and darting between sunbathing tourists.

In the summer sun, her dark curls got lighter and lighter until they were more golden like mine. But the lashes which framed her deep blue eyes were as black as ever. She smiled at everyone with unshakable confidence. Nothing seemed to trouble her.

In March, when she was christened at St Bride's church on Fleet Street, she stared up at the vicar with trusting eyes while he sprinkled holy water on her head. She didn't cry. Not once. She looked up at him with her large, blue eyes and smiled knowingly.

* * *

At the beginning of June, a letter dropped on to the doormat. I picked it up and showed Anya the white airmail envelope and the pictures of a ballet dancer and an *electrichka* train on the Russian stamps.

I spent four frustrated days staring at Dima's Cyrillic scrawl across the checked, cream-coloured piece of paper inside. The only person in London I knew who spoke Russian was my friend William, and he was away working in Moscow.

In the end, I asked an Estonian lifeguard at the local swimming pool to translate it for me.

'It's a very nice letter,' he said encouragingly, after scanning his eyes down the two pages. Then he began to read.

Hello my darling Barbara and my little Anyutka,

At this moment, my head is bursting with thoughts and I don't even know where to start.

I think I will begin by thanking you so much, Barbara, for the pictures of our beautiful little angel. I am crazy about her. She is a miracle. My mother was kissing all the pictures when they arrived a week ago and she said that such a beautiful child is only born every hundred years. My grandmother and grandfather are very happy that they have such a beautiful granddaughter.

I can't wait to see both of you. Think of that day when we will be three of us together and I can hug and kiss the two of you.

Also, I want to meet your parents and your brother, but I'm afraid that our meeting will be very difficult because of my language problem.

But the main problem, Barbara, you know we have spoken about it a couple of times, is the money to travel to England. My monthly salary is not more than $100 and so it's hard to save anything. I don't think it will be possible for me to come this year.

I have been thinking a lot about your trip to Solikamsk and I am not sure about that. It's a very big risk for the baby's health as she is very small and four flights and the different climate would be very difficult and my mother said to ask you about it. But, however, she's missing you a lot and she can't wait for the moment that she will see you and her granddaughter.

Please think about all this, my dear, about whether you still want to come to Solikamsk or not and write to me with all your thoughts about that.

I was talking with my chief about my holiday, I can get a holiday not earlier than September. When we last spoke, I think you said that you can get holiday any time.

About myself, there is not much to write. Life is very boring and the same every day. Work, training and home. Sometimes I can relax with a friend of mine, go fishing and have a couple of beers. That's all I do.

With this weather I don't even go outside a lot. It's either snowing or raining. The temperature is zero degrees. That's all my news.

I want you, my dear, to write me a very big letter about you and about our wonderful daughter and my mother wants to hear all about your family.

Give my regards to your parents. My love and kisses to

Anyutka. Congratulations to the Queen on the occasion of her Golden Jubilee. I am kissing you many, many times.

All my friends in Solikamsk send you their love.

Boris asks a small favour. If you have a chance, could you get a magazine or album of tattoo designs?

One more time, I am kissing you again and Anyutka.

Goodbye, Dima
24.05.02

A week later, I carefully filled out a passport application form for Anya. I took her to a local photographic shop where a salesgirl took her picture with a Polaroid camera.

When the gold-embossed burgundy passport arrived one morning, I opened it to see Anya looking comically out of the page and waving an arm in the air. I telephoned Aeroflot and booked a return ticket to Moscow. There were no flights onwards to Perm. The airport had been closed for repairs.

'We'll take the train,' said Olga. 'It's the best way to travel.'

She had offered to come with me to Solikamsk, despite the fact that she had fallen madly in love since we had last seen each other. She couldn't believe it was going so well. She hadn't had much luck with men in the past.

Not long after our summer trip to Solikamsk, there had been an unfortunate incident with Dima's friend Volodya. He turned up without warning at her flat during a month-long solo tour of Moscow and St Petersburg.

His visit began well. He arrived armed with a bunch of red roses and a framed photograph he had taken of Olga during out fateful camping trip. It showed her crouching down in the sand with her camera, taking a picture of some birds.

Soon, however, it was clear he was drunk.

When Olga's mother opened the door, he marched in.

'Hello, I'm Olga's boyfriend. Has she told you about me?'

Olga made her denials out of earshot.

'I hardly know him,' she told her shocked mother. 'He is not my boyfriend.'

He said he had nowhere to go and asked if he could stay the night. Olga reluctantly agreed. Volodya believed that his conquest was complete, but while he slept on the floor of the flat, Olga shared her room with her best friend, Dasha.

The next day, vodka transformed Volodya and he pawed at Olga once again. She shouted at him and told him to leave.

'It was awful,' she recalled. 'He was so drunk. I couldn't stand it. Men are so awful.'

A few months later, however, she met a businessman in St Petersburg where she had gone to do an interview for a Russian newspaper.

It was a wonderful story. Olga left her coat and scarf on an empty chair in the marketing office she was visiting. She passed Anton in a corridor minutes later and was immediately smitten. While she went on to begin her interview, Anton returned to his desk and, unaware that the garments on it were hers, lifted the scarf to his nose, inhaled deeply and sighed: 'I have to meet the girl who wears this.'

By the time we had started planning our third visit to Solikamsk, she was talking about moving to St Petersburg and getting married, but there was one major obstacle to their love – Olga's dog.

Anton didn't share Olga's devotion to Carlos, her big, black and rust pedigree spaniel.

'Olga,' he told her, 'if you want to travel across the world, I will wait for you. If there is a new mission to the moon and you want to go, I will come and wave you off; if you want to spend six months with a tribe in deepest Africa, I will write to you every day. But I cannot live with your dog.'

For Olga, it was a terrible dilemma. On the one hand she believed that if Anton truly loved her, he would let her keep the dog. On the other, she conceded that it seemed madness to put a pet before the man she loved.

In the end, her mother cared for poor spurned Carlos during Olga's long and frequent trips to St Petersburg, and she would smother him with affection on her return.

17

We drove to Heathrow on a hot summer evening. There was only a week of August left. Anya was nearly ten months old. The pavements outside the bars were crowded with people. Couples walked hand-in-hand in the soft fading light, hanging on to the last of the summer. London was bathed in the pink gold setting sun.

Anya wriggled and squirmed on my lap before the plane took off. Eventually the sound of the engines quietened her, and when she slept her hair stuck to her clammy face like satin ribbons.

The flight cots were broken so I held her in my arms. By the time we reached Moscow, they ached from the weight of her. I carried her towards passport control. The warm night air clung to my skin. Beneath my shirt, sweat trickled down my spine.

Olga was waiting at the arrivals gate at Moscow's Sheremetyevo airport. She hadn't changed a bit. She was neat and efficient, with the same shiny dark plait trailing down her back and a fringe that curled above dark brown eyes.

'Oh Barbara, she's so lovely!' she squealed, taking hold of one of Anya's tiny pink hands.

'She looks just like a Russian baby,' she added, staring intently at her. 'You can see it in her eyes.'

She batted away the taxi drivers who buzzed around us as we walked through the airport. She had a car waiting for her. As ever, it was being driven by someone she had flagged down outside her flat. We drove to an orange-coloured block of flats near the Komsomolskaya Square dominated by Moscow's three railway stations, Kazanskiy, Yaroslavskiy and Leningradskiy. It was where Olga's mother and grandmother lived and where Olga had spent her childhood.

The apartment had been given to her grandfather in 1970, a senior Communist Party official and Red Army general, during Brezhnev's stagnant grey rule. The past lurked in the tower block's dreary brickwork. You could sense it in the dark lobby downstairs and in the lift that carried us to the tenth floor.

The sounds of dogs barking grew louder and louder as we ascended. A voice shouted to silence them. A door opened and a short, plump old lady in a floral dress and black leather slippers padded out on to the landing.

It was Olga's grandmother Zoya. Eyes squinted up at me briefly from a lined face. She looked at me in the same way Yulia's grandmother had done the previous summer. Cautious but friendly. Suspicious but curious. Baffled as to why I was there. She had a different look for Anya.

'Ah!' she cried with pleasure when she saw her. She lifted her up and kissed her and spirited her away into the apartment.

*

Olga went out to buy food. Zoya, who was eighty-four, rarely left the apartment. I went into the bathroom to wash. Olga's salary working for a British news agency in Moscow had paid for expensive Western fittings, but she hadn't been able to find a plumber to fit them. She had managed to connect the sink herself, but it hadn't been secured to the wall and wobbled alarmingly when the taps were on. There was hot water, but the shower only worked when the taps in the sink were on at the same time.

When I came out, Zoya spoke at me in fast, emphatic, incomprehensible Russian, occasionally pointing at Anya. I nodded at carefully timed intervals and smiled politely and wished that Olga would hurry up and return.

When she did, Zoya told her: 'I like the *Anglichanka*. She shows respect. She doesn't answer back like you do.'

'For her you are the perfect guest,' said Olga.

Olga's mother arrived from work. Eugenia was petite like Olga but her long brown hair was swept into an elegant chignon. It was hard to believe they were mother and daughter. Together, they behaved like sisters. There was a whiff of rivalry between them. It was Zoya who was in charge. She watched her two girls running around trying to please her and competing for her affection with satisfaction in her glittering eyes.

Eugenia baked chicken smothered in sour cream and poured sweet Georgian wine into our glasses, and we sat down at the table.

The women looked down disapprovingly at my bare-footed, bare-headed, bare-armed daughter.

'She lets the girl crawl on the floor!' said Zoya, with a look of horror on her face.

'Why doesn't she put socks on the baby?' asked Eugenia, baffled.

'It's her baby,' Olga told them. 'I'm sure she knows best.'

'Of course she doesn't know best,' retorted Zoya. 'How can she possibly know best? It's only her first child.'

Olga turned to me.

'If Anton and I ever have a baby, I want to be a modern mother just like you are with Anya,' she said. 'I don't care what my mother and grandmother say.' Unable to understand her speaking in English, Eugenia and Zoya ignored her, unaware that she was plotting against them.

Olga's early childhood had been spent wrapped up in several layers of warm winter clothing even during the stifling Moscow summers. Other children were banned from visiting for fear that they might bring infection and disease with them.

She was shut up alone apart from her mother and grandmother. Her parents had already separated when her mother realised she was pregnant.

'My mother wanted to have an abortion and bought all the necessary medication,' said Olga, 'but my Granny said that the first abortion is always the most dangerous and persuaded her to keep it.'

Eugenia tried to keep the pregnancy secret from Olga's father, but he found out and the next few months were filled with arguments. Zoya claimed the ensuing stress meant Olga was born with an 'imperfect nervous system'. She cried all the time and would not sleep for more than forty minutes.

When Olga's mother and father finally divorced, he was given weekly visiting rights. But his visits didn't last for long.

'My Granny told me he used to come and read his newspaper next to my pram, paying no attention to me at all,' recalled Olga. 'I don't know whether I should believe her.'

When he next got in touch, Olga was eight. Her father thought she had just turned seven and, like all Russian children, about to start school. He wanted to take her on her first day.

Her mother laughed cynically and told him he was a year out with his dates.

The last time her mother heard from him, Olga was twelve.

'He told my mother: "A daughter needs a father from this age." My mother said it was too late.'

When Olga was sixteen, she changed her name from the one her father had bequeathed her – Antonova – to her mother's family name, Lebedeva.

After her grandfather Ivan died, her mother and grandmother found they didn't need a man to support them. Eugenia worked in a government department responsible for the Five Year plans for the Soviet Union's industrial growth. In the 1970s, she worked as an operator of one of the first IBM computers to arrive in Moscow.

But while her mother was perfectly content, Olga found it hard to forget her father entirely. She didn't even know what he looked like. Her mother had no photographs of him.

Once, she decided to try and find him.

She knew his surname was Antonov and that he was the same age as her mother. She knew his first name, Sergiy, from her own patronymic, Sergiyevna. But she didn't know his patronymic until she was asked for it while filling out some official documents.

She asked her mother, who told her it was Vitaliyevich.

Now Olga had all the information she needed.

She searched for him on a Moscow database and discovered he was living in one of the most prestigious residential areas of Moscow, not far from Vladimir Putin and Boris Yeltsin. The records showed that she had a half-brother just a few months younger than she was, and a sister she had never met.

But she never went to see him. She couldn't bear the thought that he would think she was after his money, and she was afraid that if her mother found out she would never forgive her.

If Zoya and Eugenia thought men were a waste of time, babies were another matter entirely.

'Anyinky, malinky, horoshinky,' chanted her grandmother, holding a grinning Anya in her arms. 'Little Anya, little one, little beauty.'

The women tutted at the madness of taking a nine-month-old baby halfway across Russia.

'No good can come of your relationship with this man,' said Zoya, shaking her head wisely and staring at me with pity in her face.

'She's certainly brave,' said her mother.

Her grandmother laughed and poured more wine for us.

'She is the wife of a December man,' she declared.

She told us a story. It was about a group of Russian aristocrats – the *Dekabristi*, the Decembrists – who plotted to overthrow Tsar Nicholas I in 1825.

Russia's first democratic movement was formed by army officers who had fought in the Napoleonic Wars. During months in Europe, they warmed to the liberal ideas they encountered there and zealously carried them home.

They marched on Senate Square in St Petersburg on 14 December 1825, but their treacherous plot was discovered. They were crushed by artillery fire and the 120 that survived the attempted coup were sent into exile in Siberia.

Determined to blot out his faithless subjects, Tsar Nicholas passed a new law allowing the convicts' wives to be regarded as widows and to remarry without divorce.

But they rejected his offer, abandoned their luxurious, palatial homes, gave up their privileges as nobles, and travelled by sleigh and carriage across Russia with their children to share in their husbands' grim fate.

One of the first to leave was Countess Yekaterina Trubetskaya, who rapidly set off a day after her husband Sergiy Trubetskoy in July 1826.

She was pursued by bandits in the Taiga, her carriage broke down on the ice of the River Yenisei, and at one stage she was detained for nine months. When she finally made it to Blagodatsk near Lake Baikal, she joined forces with Princess Maria Volkonskaya, another Decembrist's wife, and the pair rented a tiny house with rooms so cold that there was frost on the inside of the walls. At night, as the temperature dropped, their hair would freeze to the bed.

'They were prepared to go to the ends of the earth for their men,' concluded Zoya.

She lifted her glass: 'To the *Anglichanka*, wife of a December man.'

After we had drunk the sweet, amber liquid, her face became serious and she took my hand in hers.

'It's madness,' she said, shaking her head. 'You have your baby, now you should forget this Russian man.'

*

That night, Olga and I shared the bedroom and lay side by side in narrow beds. She whispered across to me in the darkness.

'You mustn't listen to them,' she said softly. 'It's their dream for me just to get pregnant and give them the baby to bring up without a man around. But I won't do it.'

I felt Anya's warm little body nuzzled up next to me and thought of Dima. I thought about how little he really knew about me. I hadn't seen him for over a year. His daughter was lying beside me but he had never seen her. Zoya and Eugenia thought men were worthless and yet I was pinning my hopes on a man I hardly knew. I wondered what I really expected from him. If he was capable of rescuing me, it was unlikely that he was aware of it.

That night my dreams were crowded with faces. Zoya and Eugenia shouted and lectured me. Mr B smiled at me knowingly. Dima stared, untroubled, into the distance. I didn't know which way to turn. When Anya's cries woke me in the morning, my head felt thick with tiredness and nerves.

* * *

In the afternoon after saying goodbye to Zoya and Eugenia, we stood on the street outside the apartment block and waited while Olga tried to flag down a passing car.

Eventually, an off-duty government driver pulled over in a glossy black Lada. His face dropped when he saw me standing behind Olga with Anya in my arms and a buggy and several large bags, but he agreed to take us for ten dollars. We drove to the station in luxury, sitting on shiny soft leather seats.

Kazanskiy station was swamped by noisy crowds. Men stood outside smoking and swigging from bottles of beer. Beggars sat on the pavement outside. The road outside was cluttered with stationary cars, dropping people off, picking people up. We struggled to carry our bags and push Anya's buggy up the steps.

The *provodnitsa* standing by the door to our carriage examined our three tickets before showing us to a compartment with bunk beds on either side. Olga deftly stowed our bags and the pushchair under the long, red banquette seats.

In return for twenty roubles each, the *provodnitsa* brought us blankets and pillows and we spread ourselves out across the two opposite-facing bottom bunks.

Seconds before the train jolted into life, the compartment door slid open and a young man in smart jeans and a denim shirt walked in and stood glaring at us.

'Two girls and a baby?' he told the *provodnitsa* at his side. 'You've got to be joking.'

She shrugged and told him there was nothing else and he told Olga to move to one of the top bunks. She refused with a snap of anger and he climbed the ladder above her muttering: 'You girls!'

Bogdan Mazov was on his way home from a mathematics convention in Beijing and was travelling to Nizhny Novgorod, where he was a lecturer at the University of Architecture and Civil Engineering.

Curiosity got the better of him. I could see him listening to us as we talked in English.

'Is it true all the cattle in Britain are dying?' he asked

eagerly, hanging perilously over the edge of the top bunk.

'Did your government really kill Princess Diana?'

Hour by hour, the train rushed past forests of pine and birch trees with no relief between stations. Moscow's stuffy air became cool and clean as we swept eastwards. We left summer behind.

The light softened. Green trees were replaced by a sea of russet, brown and gold. The first exhilarating tendrils of cold trickled into the compartment. The temperature inside dropped. I reached up and closed the sliding vent at the top of the window.

* * *

The train was a hive of activity.

Gypsies and Georgians walked up and down the train corridor offering pies and crystals and jewellery for sale.

Each time the train stopped, passengers hopped on and off to buy beer and cigarettes and soft toys imported from China from vendors on the platform.

Olga's mother had sent us off well equipped for the journey and Olga produced large brown envelopes containing boiled eggs, roast chicken, tomatoes, cucumber and slices of bread. We invited Bogdan to share our meal.

While we ate, he told us about his one-year-old son, Artyom, waiting for him at home, and the theory he was working on with several other mathematicians that statistics would eventually be used to predict human behaviour.

'Even free will becomes predictable eventually,' he said.

We asked our attendant to bring us tea. She had changed out of the neat grey suit she was wearing when we boarded the train, and padded down the carpeted corridor in her slippers carrying three white china mugs.

While Anya drifted off to sleep, we argued until the forests sweeping past were swallowed up by darkness. I thought of Dima. In a few hours he would be setting off to meet us in Perm in his friend's car.

I wondered what he was thinking.

It was a year since I had last seen him and I had already managed as a mother for nine months without him.

She was his daughter and yet he had never seen her. Again, I thought how little he knew about my life.

I looked down at Anya sleeping.

I thought: *One day I will tell you about this. The very moment you first set eyes on your father. And you will ask me so many questions about it and I will try to remember everything exactly as it is.*

I touched her curls with my hand and rubbed my nose against her warm, sticky face. I slept.

I heard Bogdan leave in the early hours of the morning. While Olga slept in the bunk opposite me, I watched his tall silhouette climb down from the top bunk in the darkness and head off home to his wife and baby son. I wondered what their house looked like and if his wife would be awake when he got there.

His place was taken by a teenage girl, who undressed quietly and stepped up the ladder. But by the time the sun came up, she too had gone.

18

The train slowly pulled into the station at Perm and my eyes scanned the crowds on the platform for a glimpse of Dima.

I didn't see him until we had almost stopped. He was clutching a bunch of red carnations in one hand and a pink rabbit in the other and was looking up and down the train. I was relieved I had seen him first. It made me feel less vulnerable somehow.

He looked older, as if he had lived through more than a year since I last saw him. He was thinner and his dark hair was swept with flecks of grey.

I looked at Anya, who had just woken from her afternoon nap, yawning gently and reaching her arms out to be picked up, oblivious to the momentous meeting that was about to take place.

We stepped from the carriage and Olga shouted to him. He walked straight towards us, took Anya into his arms and kissed her gently and firmly. She stared at him with her head on one side and grabbed at his nose, before pawing the rabbit he placed in her hands. He looked at me, smiling. His brilliant blue eyes were shining.

In Ulitsa Lenina, Natalya was waiting, watching for us. I could see her leaning out from the enclosed balcony when the car pulled into the unmade road leading to their apartment block.

She ran down the stairs and within seconds she appeared at the big rusting iron door. She let out a cry of joy and relief at finally seeing her granddaughter.

She scooped her up and carried her upstairs. Anya screamed out in the pitch dark stairwell and Natalya ignored her wails with a confident laugh which said: 'Don't be silly. We are family.'

They had prepared everything in the flat down to the last detail. In the corner of Dima's room, next to the giant picture of the stormy coastline was a wooden cot that he and Boris had made.

Inside, Natalya had placed a thick quilt and a red blanket, covered with beige-coloured pine trees which had been Dima's as a child.

She had bought new flannels and towels and a set of blue plastic whales for the bath, a wooden dove to hang above Anya while she slept, and a wooden horseshoe to keep away evil spirits.

Anya crawled around the three-roomed flat, happy to be free at last from the confines of trains and cars. She reached out to grab the tail of Natalya's long-haired white cat, Byelka.

Dima and Natalya watched her avidly. There was love and wonder in their faces.

We marked our arrival with bottles of sweet wine from the

Caucasus and bread, meat and cucumber before Natalya began passing Olga her coat and shoes and put on her own.

They were staying the night at a dacha belonging to Natalya's friends Galina and Darya.

'Tonight,' she told Olga, 'we will both sleep there. The three of them should be alone together.'

Olga turned to me.

'See you in the morning,' she said with a knowing grin on her face.

Dima and I undressed and climbed on to his cramped sofa bed. He buried his face in my hair and asked me if I loved him. At that moment – the three of us lying in one room; our breaths mingling – it was easy to say that I did.

When Anya woke in the middle of the night, I lifted her into the bed between us and we slept with an arm each around her.

19

Summer had tipped over into autumn in Solikamsk. Brittle leaves swept across the road and crackled underfoot. Men and women had already begun purposefully striding along the pavements with their heads down in readiness for winter's icy blasts. In Revolution Square, the hotel looked the same as ever. Grey, bland, immovable, empty. Untouched by the chain of events that had begun in one of its rooms. I looked up at the windows on the top floor and counted along to find mine. I wanted to carry Anya up the stairs and lie alongside her on the shiny turquoise bed. For just a minute, I wanted to go back to where it all began. I wanted to sit there and try and take it all in.

Even before presenting her to Boris and Yulia and Katya and Vladimir Tyshchenko, I had a strange feeling that she should already know them.

At Yulia's grandmother's dacha, Boris tickled Anya under the chin and Yulia's strong arms lifted her out of mine. She showed her to Katya. 'Beautiful baby,' they said in English, over and over again.

'Ah! Valinskaya! Valinskaya!' cried Vladimir Tyshchenko in his deep voice when he saw that Anya had the dark curls and blue-grey eyes of her father.

He marvelled to Yulia: 'Horoshinky, da? Horoshinky.'

In the garden, the flowers were already withering at the first cold touches of winter.

The orange tiger lilies had faded into brown stalks, but the bushes bristled with raspberries and blackcurrants. I popped them into Anya's trusting mouth and she pulled a face as the dark red juice dripped down her chin.

The sun set, streaking the sky with pink and amber. We sat around a wooden table in the garden eating pork shashlyk and dried fish swilled down with beer.

I drank vodka with the men while Katya pushed Anya around the garden in her buggy and Yulia crushed mint and basil to scent the banya.

Dima and I went in first. In seconds he was naked and looked across the dressing room towards me. I peeled my clothes off reluctantly and slowly, cringing at the thought of my crinkled post-pregnancy stomach. Dima stared at me quizzically, with his head on one side. I stopped undressing, folded my arms and stared back.

'You don't want me to look?' he asked.

I replied matter-of-factly: it was impossible to pretend otherwise.

'No.' I said, with an awkward smile. 'I don't want you to look.'

He shrugged, opened the door to the banya and

disappeared through a wall of herb-scented steam.

Without his eyes on me, I undressed quickly and followed him in.

It was dark and silent inside. There was so much steam, it was hard to breathe.

I looked at him, eyes closed, leaning back against the side of the banya, naked, unashamed and untroubled. His lean body shimmered in the hot moist air and he sighed.

'It's good,' he said in English, without opening his eyes.

When we emerged pink and glowing, Yulia asked if she could take Anya in with her.

Dima nodded. When I protested, he held up his hand to silence me. He was keen that his daughter should undergo this rite of passage.

Anya was passed into Yulia's arms. She carried her into the dressing room and took off her warm snowsuit.

The banya had cooled slightly by the time she was cere-moniously carried inside. She cried and waved her arms at me through the closing door and I fought the urge to help her escape.

* * *

In the morning we went to buy food for Anya. Fidel and Boris drove us in an old van from the prison. There were no seatbelts in the back. Dima held Anya on his lap and I tried to stop worrying about how unsafe it was.

The zebra-print car seat I had brought from England had proved to be useless. There were no seatbelts in the back of any of the cars we had been in and it was illegal for children to travel in the front of a car. No one was prepared to risk being stopped by the police.

When we stopped, Olga and I jumped out of the sliding side door. The building in front of us didn't look like a shop. There were no signs and no front windows. Inside, most of the shelves were empty. Olga asked for baby food and a woman in a white coat unlocked a cupboard revealing small, unmarked tins, covered in rust. The women pointed at them and then unlocked a second cupboard and a third. Olga translated: 'These ones are chicken. This cupboard contains beef. And this one is brain.'

We left empty-handed.

At the pharmacy, another woman showed us a selection of powdered baby milk with 'live cultures'.

Olga looked baffled when I asked if we could buy fresh cow's milk instead.

'Perhaps if we tried a farm,' she suggested.

In the end I bought chicken to go with the pasta I had brought from London, and apples and yoghurt. I bought the powdered milk with the live cultures but when I made it up it was thin and white, nothing like the thick creamy formula milk I gave Anya at home.

'It's very good for the baby,' said Olga when I turned my nose up at it. 'It's very popular among Russian mothers.'

Reluctantly I gave it to Anya, half expecting her to spit it out. Despite my doubts, she happily sucked on her bottle.

She seemed completely at home in her new surroundings. She was unfazed by so many new faces and the strange rhythms of the day. She crawled around the flat after Byelka's tantalising white tail. She dabbled her fingers in the emergency buckets of water Natalya kept under the kitchen table.

At home in London, each day ended with a warm, lavender-scented bath. I'd rub olive oil into her little pink body until her eyes drooped with pleasure and tiredness.

At Dima's apartment, giving her a bath in the deep, cracked, rust-stained tub was out of the question. Natalya only ever used it for washing clothes. And every time I took Anya into the cramped, dark bathroom she screamed in terror and arched her back away from me.

Natalya bought a large red plastic bowl at the local market. Anya could just fit in it if her legs were curled up. She protested when I lowered her towards the soapy water. It wasn't even deep enough to cover her legs. In the end I stood her up and splashed water over her grubby little body. She smelt sweet, like a hamster in sawdust. She screamed and cried and I worked quickly.

Her arrival in Solikamsk precipitated a steady flow of visits from relatives. She was picked up and set down, passed from lap to lap, kissed and tickled and showered with gifts: a small wooden ladle, a set of matrioshka dolls, a pink rabbit which squeaked in an American accent when its stomach was pressed: 'Some bunny loves you!'

The first to come were Dima's uncle Tolya and his wife Tatiana, who looked nothing like the slim, timid-looking bride I had once seen in a wedding photograph in Natalya's album. She was jolly and robust and her tweed jacket was buttoned tightly across her large bosom.

They arrived with their shy sixteen-year-old daughter Masha.

'Why doesn't she put socks on the baby?' Tatiana asked Natalya. 'She'll catch cold.'

Tolya swung Anya around the room until she screwed up her eyes and squealed with exhilaration.

'I think she is hungry,' said Tatiana, taking a banana from the table of food Natalya had laid out in the living room. 'Is she being fed properly?'

Anya snatched at the fruit and crammed it into her mouth, while Tatiana raised her eyebrows and gave Natalya a sideways look which said: 'I told you so! The *Anglichanka* doesn't know how to feed her baby.'

Such criticism was nothing compared to the onslaught I risked every time I stepped outside the apartment.

'You haven't got her dressed properly! The poor child will freeze to death!' was the sort of greeting I learned to expect when I took Anya out.

Babushki wrapped up in coats and scarves would cross the road with their heavy bags of shopping to tell me off, point at my hatless baby and educate me on how to care for her properly.

'Why doesn't she have anything covering her head?'

Motherhood, it seemed, was an art form at which I would only become proficient after years of experience and several children.

When Natalya's friends trooped round to the flat to see her granddaughter, their criticisms were no less harsh.

'I know,' Natalya would tell them. 'You think they'd know better in a country like England.'

Olga thought it was hysterical.

'They're not really worried about the baby,' she explained. 'It's just a way of showing that they know best.'

Once, when Anya had been fractious and prone to tears, Natalya declared that she had been exposed to too many people.

'They pass on evil spirits to her,' she said, walking into the kitchen and taking a small bottle of water out of the cupboard.

'Holy water,' she said, rubbing some of it on Anya's forehead.

Olga, who had been nursing a sore eye all day, asked to be anointed next. Natalya took mouthfuls of the sacred liquid, pursed her lips and blew it across her face in a fine mist.

'You know,' Olga commented later, 'it really has worked.'

After a few days, I couldn't stand it any more. I gave in.

Anya was wrapped up in her snow suit and her brown curls were squashed under the red hat Natalya had bought her in the market.

One evening she was joined by another baby girl, one-year-old Polina. The two girls babbled at each other on the rug in the living room. Language was no barrier to them.

Polina's father, Volodya, an officer in the local militia, worked with Dima and he and his elfin-faced blonde wife arrived on our second evening.

'What a beautiful child,' said Irina. 'Why doesn't she have any socks on?'

Polina was wearing two pairs of socks – as well as woollen tights, trousers and a jumper. Even inside the apartment, her mother refused to take off the knitted hat tied tightly under her chin. She stared in disbelief at Anya crawling around the room in a t-shirt and nappy.

They lived in army barracks in Solikamsk, all three of them

in one room, sharing a kitchen and bathroom with twenty others. Polina's five-year-old brother, Pavel, had been sent to live with his grandparents to make room for the new baby.

I thought about our one-bedroom flat and Anya's smooth beechwood cot next to my bed at home. I resolved to stop worrying about the fact that we didn't have a garden and couldn't afford to move.

'The three of us sleep in one bed,' explained Irina. She added with a laugh, 'with the washing drying above us'.

It got late. We put Polina and Anya in the cot together and they slept.

Soon, Irina explained, she would have slightly more space at home. Volodya was going to Chechnya for six months. She and Polina would have the bed to themselves.

We swapped childbirth experiences. Like Anya, both her children had been delivered by Caesarean.

'In Russian hospitals,' she explained, 'most babies are.'

I told her about birthing pools and birthing balls, homeo-pathy and aromatherapy, acupuncture and hypnotism, and she looked at me in astonishment.

'Don't you have pain relief?' she asked, and looked stunned when I tried to explain that in England most women hoped they would manage without.

When it was time for them to leave, Irina kissed me on both cheeks.

'I didn't realise you would be so normal,' she said. 'At first I thought you were a bit strange, but now I think you are really just like us.'

A few days later, when Natalya took Anya out in her buggy to the market, she was approached in the street by a doctor from the local children's hospital.

'My goodness, that is the healthiest looking child I have ever seen,' she told her. 'What is her mother's secret?'

'My daughter-in-law is English and the baby is being brought up in London,' replied Natalya proudly.

The doctor said: 'Could you ask her what book she uses? It must be a good one. My daughter is expecting her first child, I would like to give it to her.'

The doctor scribbled her telephone number on a piece of paper and thrust it into Natalya's hand before continuing on her way.

I had been vindicated at last.

20

Soft, silent rain covered Solikamsk in a mist. The air was cold and damp. Mushroom-picking season had arrived, and half the town appeared to be arming themselves with wicker baskets and driving out into the countryside in search of them.

Natalya had already been to the forest with friends and returned, proudly showing off the plump brown and grey jewels she had plucked from the moist black earth, but she refused to tell Dima where she had found them.

'Find your own mushrooms,' she said as she began cleaning and sorting them in the kitchen. 'And don't think I'll be pickling them for you. You can do them yourself.'

Later, she fried some of hers in butter and stirred in sour cream. They tasted earthy and slippery and musty and warm.

'I found them beneath a forest tree,' she whispered to Olga, when Dima was out of earshot. 'Hundreds of them, nestling in a carpet of emerald-coloured moss.'

Dima, Boris and Yulia joined the mass exodus to the forest the following day. Olga, Anya and I didn't go with them.

'You can't possibly take the baby there, she'll be eaten alive by the insects,' said Natalya.

In the morning, Dima pulled some old, fusty army fatigues from the back of his wardrobe and hastily dressed. Boris's car pulled up on the street below and he sounded the horn. Dima shouted to him from the balcony before kissing me goodbye and running out of the door.

I followed him out of the bedroom and caught sight of my face in a mirror in the hallway. My unwashed hair looked dull and greasy. My face looked pasty and puffy. I gazed briefly back at my reflection, shuddered and turned away.

Olga called a taxi. We were going to see Boris and Yulia's daughter, Katya. She was thirteen now. Mushroom-picking with her parents didn't hold much excitement for her. She preferred to stay at home or hang around with her friends outside the local shop. We asked the driver to take us to the Kapolev's apartment in Ulitsa Parizhkoy Kommuny. He dropped us off at the bottom of the road and we walked the rest of the way up broken concrete stairs leading through the ascending rows of identical grey blocks.

Katya's heart-shaped face appeared around the door when we knocked. We kissed and hugged her and she asked if she could hold Anya.

'Come and see this!' called Olga. She had gone into the bathroom. 'They have a shower in here.'

I went to look. In the corner of the bathroom, next to a disconnected washing machine, was a shower cubicle.

'It's new,' said Katya. 'You can have a go if you want.'

Olga went first and when she emerged, her long dark hair

like a wet cape around her shoulders, I took my turn.

After days of washing out of saucepans, I could barely contain my excitement. Hot water rained down on my shoulders. I washed my hair, but even when there were no traces of shampoo left, I didn't switch the shower off. I stood beneath the steady stream and washed away the dust and the dirt.

When I turned the taps off, I could hear another woman's voice in the apartment. I dried myself, got dressed and went to see who was there.

In the sitting room stood a tall, thin, wolf-like woman. She had short, spiky bleached hair and baggy, stonewashed jeans. Her face was long and angular.

'This is Boris's sister, Larissa,' said Olga.

She added with a giggle: 'It's Dima's ex-wife!'

Larissa began speaking in broken English.

'Please understand that it was a false kind of marriage,' she said. 'There was never anything between us. It was just on paper.'

Before she left, she pressed a business card into my hand.

'I met your ex-wife today,' I told Dima later. He had returned from the forest with an enormous basket of mushrooms and a bunch of large white daisies which he gave to me.

'Lara?' he asked calmly. He shrugged his shoulders and walked away.

Later, I took the business card out of my bag and saw 'Larissa Valinskaya' displayed in bold red letters across it.

Despite their false marriage and divorce, it felt strange that another woman still carried his name.

21

We had been in Solikamsk for a week and still Dima, Anya and I had not been out together – just the three of us.

I remembered the weary, disillusioned faces of the young mothers I had seen out alone with their babies when I had visited the previous summer.

When I asked Dima about it, he shrugged: 'There's nowhere to go.'

'Just a walk, then,' I suggested. 'Can we do that?'

He agreed, but with a look that said he was humouring me. In a town where negotiating the crumbling pavements meant frequently crossing the street, walking was a necessity, not something you did for pleasure.

A cold wind whipped up the dust on the stony road outside the block. Between us we carried Anya up broken concrete steps and past a derelict playground. The rusting frames of old swings were covered with carpets being beaten clean by weary-faced housewives.

Dima asked me to wait at the edge of a small market a few

streets away. He disappeared down an avenue of blue metal huts with tiny hatch windows and re-emerged with a bottle of beer.

'You didn't get one for me,' I said. I didn't want one, but it annoyed me that he hadn't asked.

He sighed and went back for another one.

Carrying our bottles, we walked through the streets. I got out my camera and took photographs: Anya wrapped up in a warm fleece coat. Anya next to the blue, white and gold-tipped Orthodox Church of the Saviour. Anya in front of a vodka kiosk where old women with wrinkled brown stockings around their ankles and garish scarves over their heads sat clutching bags of shopping.

We carried the buggy across a railway line and down a steep bank that sloped towards the Usolka river. I took out my camera again, this time pointing it at Dima holding Anya in his arms. We sat on the large rocks at the edge of the river and Dima finished the rest of my beer.

He smoked a cigarette and he asked me how much Anya's pushchair had cost. It hadn't been particularly expensive but the amount I had paid was almost exactly a month's salary for him. He nodded emotionlessly when I told him. His face looked hard and grey.

He stared silently across the Usolka, his shoulders turned away from me. It began to rain softly. He slowly rose to his feet and helped me carry Anya back up the steep bank. We walked back home in silence.

Natalya's sister and niece were patiently waiting for us to return.

Flame-haired Ludmilla and tall elegant ballet-dancing accountancy student Anastasia gave Anya a traditional hand-painted wooden spoon to mark the arrival of her first teeth. She grabbed it with interest and lifted it straight to her mouth.

Dima announced that he was going out for the evening.

'All these women together. It's not interesting for me,' he said when I protested. 'What will I talk about?'

'Let him go,' said Olga. 'It's normal for a man not to want to be in the company of so many women.'

I thought she was wrong. I stubbornly told Dima: 'It's not interesting for me to meet your relatives either. I'm coming with you.'

'No problem,' he said.

Dima calmed his furious mother by promising that we would be gone only an hour, and Luda and Nastya said they would wait for us to return.

We left Anya and set off for Volodya's, a couple of streets away, stopping off on the way to buy beer and dried fish.

Volodya had recovered from his failed bid to woo Olga in Moscow and, in the twelve months that had passed since, had found another Olga, a taller, younger version.

In that time, she had fallen pregnant and they had married. He had bought a one-bedroom apartment on the top floor of one of the blocks of flats opposite Dima's and had furiously begun renovating it in time for the arrival of their baby.

When Dima and I arrived clutching two large bottles of beer and three dried fish, he and his older brother Sergiy were stripping the walls in a sitting room identical to Dima's.

The air was thick with sawdust. Carved wooden doors were propped up in the hallway, ready to be fitted.

There was no sign of Volodya's new bride. Olga was in hospital. Scans had shown that her baby was too small for its due date four months later, and the doctors decided both mother and child needed fattening up.

She telephoned from her hospital bed while we were there, and through the doorway of the sitting room I could hear Volodya's soothing voice as he spoke tenderly to her.

I looked at Dima across the table between us. I wondered if it had ever occurred to him that I needed someone to look after me. He didn't raise his eyes to meet mine.

He filled my glass with beer along with the others, but when I spoke to him in English, he snapped at me with irritation in his eyes: 'In Russian please Barbara. I am not English man.'

An hour passed quickly. We finished the beer and the extra bottles that Dima and Sergiy had gone to get from the shop beneath the flats. It was clear that what had begun as a quick break from work was not going to stop there.

When I asked Dima about it, he shrugged: 'No problem. Don't worry, be happy.'

I thought of Ludmilla and Nastya sitting patiently waiting, until it became impossible to believe that we were returning. I imagined them sighing, getting up and saying goodbye to Natalya, Olga and Anya before walking up towards the main road and waiting at the bus stop.

I asked Dima: 'What about Luda and Nastya?'

He said: 'It's not important.'

By midnight, the men had run out of beer and fish. Empty bottles and piles of fish skeletons and scaly, leathery skin covered the table. I told Dima I wanted to go, but he insisted that I didn't walk back to the apartment through the dark streets my own.

'It's not safe,' he said. 'We'll leave in a minute.'

When he wasn't looking, I took a cigarette from the packet inside his coat pocket and reached back in for some matches.

I went out on to the balcony and smoked it. I breathed in deeply. It was the first cigarette I had touched since I had thought I was pregnant. I wanted to feel the relief they had once given me.

In a second, the chemicals I inhaled rushed to my head. I held on to the side of the balcony and felt waves of nausea sweep over me. I threw the cigarette on to the street below and waited for the dizziness to pass with my head in my hands. My mouth tasted of strong tea and burnt toast. In the street below, two men were fighting. A *babushka* came out on to one of the balconies opposite to scream at them. I saw myself standing there on the rusty balcony and shuddered at the thought of it all.

I thought of Anya, asleep in the cot in Dima's room. Luda and Anastasia would have given up on the possibility that Dima and I would be coming back, and gone home by now. Natalaya would have left to go to her temporary bed at her friend's house. Olga would be asleep on the sofa.

I didn't want to be there. I was tired of searching. I longed to be at home.

Back inside the apartment, Volodya put a tape into the VCR. It was his wedding video.

'One minute please, Barbara,' he told me. 'I want you to look my beautiful Olga. Just quickly please.'

But the large bottle of vodka he placed on the table threatened something else.

I lay on the sofa near the television while Dima, Volodya and Sergiy sat around the table in the corner of the room. Occasionally, Volodya stood up to commentate on a particular moment from the video.

Volodya's bride appeared in cascades of white lace, her long dark brown hair elaborately coiled on top of her head. Despite her tall frame and tight-fitting dress it was almost impossible to detect the already-swelling belly which was partly covered by the bouquet in her hands. She looked happy enough to burst.

She and Volodya exchanged their vows at the ZAGs office in Solikamsk, where Dima had married Boris's sister Lara.

The next scene showed them making a grand entrance into an enormous room. Streamers and flowers covered the ceilings. A giant disco ball revolved above them. Olga's tearful mother stepped forward to present them with salt and bread as custom dictated. Crowds of friends and relatives clapped and cheered them and demanded to see them kiss.

After the reception, Olga's family packed into two cars, one driven by Volodya and the other by Olga's father, and they headed off in convoy with their tents in the boot.

At the end of the first day, they camped at the edge of a vast, emerald green field framed by silver birches. It didn't appear to be the kind of honeymoon night that most newly-weds enjoyed. I saw Olga sleeping under a brown blanket, her younger sisters and brother lying next to her, childishly laughing and pulling faces. Volodya slept fully clothed on the back seat of his car. He smiled for the camera before opening the door and stumbling out into the July sunshine.

My tired, heavy eyes began to close. The effort of keeping them open made them water. The screen in front of me looked blurred and hazy.

Over the next few days, the newly-weds made their way south-east through central Russia. I watched them swimming in the Volga river. Olga gently eased herself into the cold water while her younger sister and Volodya wrestled with each other until they fell in from the bank.

In Volgograd, they walked softly hand-in-hand through the Hall of Military Glory, dwarfed by the circular walls and thousands of names of the Russian soldiers who died defending the former Stalingrad from the Germans.

Afterwards they drove to a friend's house in a village near Kazan and sat in a white summer kitchen built at the bottom of the garden. They held up fresh dill and chives to the camera. The table in front of them was covered with cherries and currants, bread, chicken and sour cream. The family drank a toast to Olga and Volodya and their unborn baby, and I saw the sated look on Olga's face.

When the tape came to an end, almost all the vodka on the table had gone. I looked at my watch. It was 3 a.m.

The flat was silent when we got back. Anya was fast asleep in her cot, one hand clasping the pink rabbit Tolya and Tanya had given her. There was no sound from Olga behind the closed door of the sitting room.

I climbed into Dima's bed, desperate for the relief of sleep. It came, in a thick, heavy wave. I thought about the perfect simplicity of Volodya and Olga's big white wedding and the look on Olga's face in the garden near Kazan. I wondered what it was like to feel so certain about another person. Inside, I felt flimsy and fallible.

Then I thought about the cries that would signal the start to the next day.

When they came three hours later, I ached with tiredness. Dima stirred briefly but slept on, undisturbed by the morning yells of his daughter, and when I had left the bed he groaned and stretched himself across it. He pulled the covers up over himself and turned over to face the wall.

I stared at his back resentfully. I remembered the times in the hotel in Revolution Square when he had left me to go to work, pausing to stroke my hair from my face and kiss me goodbye.

When he woke up several hours later, he walked the few steps from his room to the sofa in the sitting room, without a word. He lay down and pointed the remote control at the television in the corner of the room. The screen burst into life with a loud click. Russia's answer to Chris Tarrant was presenting *Who Wants to Be a Millionaire?*

Dima was wearing the brown velour dressing gown he always wore at home. It was belted tightly at the waist with a woven leather belt. I broke off from playing with Anya and her *matrioshka* dolls to stare at him. He looked thin, old and weary. His hair seemed more flecked with grey than ever.

I thought about the letter he had sent to me in June: *About myself, there is not much to write. Life is very boring and the same every day. Work, training and home. Sometimes I can relax with a friend, go fishing and have a couple of beers, that's all I do.*

His eyes were fixed on the screen. He was oblivious to Anya, to me and to Olga who was quietly reading in the corner.

The look on his face frightened me. It was empty. Meaningless. I wondered whether the strength and stoicism I had once found so attractive was, in fact, his defeated spirit.

Was that what Olga had meant when she said: 'Only when you lower your expectations can you really be content'?

The phone rang on a small table next to the sofa. Without even moving his body, Dima stretched out his arm to pick it up and answered with a bored – 'Da?'

When he had finished, he got off the sofa and disappeared into the bedroom. When he emerged minutes later, he was dressed.

'I go out,' he said. This time, I didn't bother to ask where he was going. I nodded without looking up. He carefully brushed his hair in the mirror in the hallway, put on his coat and left. The door slammed shut behind him.

I talked to Olga about it. I asked if she thought it was the Russian way, or just Dima.

'He doesn't know any other life,' she said gently. 'I don't think he dreams of anything better than this.'

An hour later, the telephone rang. Olga answered it. It was Dima.

'They've arrested the man who attacked him in February,' she said. 'He says he'll be at the Militia office all day.'

* * *

We went shopping.

Olga and I walked into town with Anya in the buggy, negotiating our way around the cracked pavements, zig-zagging our way back and forth across the road to avoid piles of rubble and broken concrete.

The wind blew in gusts between the apartment blocks. The dust hurt our eyes. I pulled Anya's hat down low over her face.

In the centre of Solikamsk, men in black leather caps sat at plastic tables drinking vodka next to a little kiosk.

In the indoor market, I bought pirate Russian videos for Anya, old-fashioned cartoons. There was one about some penguins that Olga remembered from her childhood and an old 1950s animation about a flying horse.

Olga spotted a garlic press on a second-hand stall.

'What do you think it's for?' she asked me. When I told her, she thought it was ingenious. She decided to buy it for her mother.

'I will have to boil it first though,' she added thoughtfully. 'There might be TB on it.'

At a small jeweller's shop, we bought matching black and gold rings for three dollars and put them on. We said: 'Now we are sisters.'

We went to visit Ludmilla and Anastasia.

Their ground-floor apartment was not far from Boris and Yulia's. Mother and daughter answered the door standing side by side. Nastya wore a tight-fitting pale blue knitted dress. Her ballerina figure looked tiny and fragile. Her long black hair was pulled back into a high pony tail. Luda's lips were deep red like glossy cherries.

They drew us in and took us into a room with a table covered in a white cloth. We sat down and they brought blinis and chicken and potatoes and onions and wine.

'Where is Dima?' asked Luda.

Olga explained and they nodded sympathetically.

Luda was a divorcee. So was twenty-three-year-old Nastya.

'There's no choice in Solikamsk for someone beautiful and educated like Nastya,' said Luda, placing her hands on her daughter's bony shoulders. Her nails were sharp and red.

'Russian men are useless. I was wondering. Perhaps you could help to find an English husband for her.'

'Believe me,' I told her, 'English men aren't much better.'

On the way back to Dima's home, it began raining. Large warm droplets soaked into the dusty concrete.

We walked passed the Militia office and I tried to picture the scene inside.

'Do you think they'll hurt the man they've caught?' I asked Olga.

'Of course,' she said, laughing.

By the time we reached the apartment, it was pouring. It was so dark, it was hard to see where the dilapidated pavement rose and fell. Now and then, we stumbled. Torrents of rainwater rushed through the gutters.

Inside, Natalya was making soup in the kitchen. The air smelt warm and comforting. She took our wet clothes and hung them up to dry. She stirred sour cream into bowls of steaming soup and gave them to us. Afterwards we had tea and apple cake. Natalya put on the penguin video and played with Anya on a blanket on the floor. I lay on the sofa, full and sleepy. Olga was reading a book in Chinese. The wild rain lashed against the windows.

The telephone rang at six o'clock. Natalya answered it and passed it to Olga.

She listened, then placed her hand over the receiver.

'He's drunk,' she said. 'He says he might be very late, might not even come back until tomorrow.'

They finished talking and she hung up.

'The Militia officers have told this bad man that if he pays Dima $1,000, then the charges against him will be dropped.'

In return for this little favour, Olga explained, Dima had had to drink copious amounts of vodka with the officers involved.

'It's the Russian way,' she said, laughing at the look on my face.

She agreed that it was unlikely that Dima would get the money. It seemed impossible that anyone in Solikamsk would possess such a large amount.

Later that evening, after Natalya had retired to her friend's for the night and I had put Anya to bed, Dima staggered into the apartment. He took a hundred-dollar bill out of his pocket and placed it at the back of the drawer in the desk in his room. Without saying a word, he took a bottle of beer from the fridge and went out again.

22

Our visit was nearly over.

I was sitting in the kitchen of Dima's apartment with Anya on my knee, watching Natalya preparing salt cucumbers. She poured boiling water into large glass jars to sterilise them. The cucumbers were small and bright green and knobbly. She rolled them in salt and chopped dill and packed them side by side in glass jars with peppercorns and blackcurrant leaves. Then she filled the jars to the brim with boiling water and sealed them.

'*Solyonya ogurtsy!*' she announced, holding a jar up for me to see.

Dima had left the apartment before breakfast. He said he was going to find someone who would drive us back to Perm in two days' time.

Natalya told me about her parents, Nikolai and Marya – Kolya and Masha – Anya's great-grandparents. They lived in an apartment block on the outskirts of Solikamsk and her father wasn't well enough for visitors.

*

Nikolai Semyonovich Borschevoi, a former Major in the Red Army, was born in May 1929 in the village of Antipovka in the Voronezh region, in the south-east of Russia, half-way between Moscow and the Black Sea. His parents, Semyon Borschevoi and Irina Philipovna, had watched their country turned upside down by the Revolution of October 1917 and had adapted their lives accordingly.

Nikolai, who knew nothing other than the Bolshevik way, married a Ukrainian girl, Marya Sergiyevna Kuzmenko, a year younger than himself, and they spent their married life moving around the Soviet Union according to the whims of Stalin's Red Army generals.

Natalya was their eldest child. Natalya Nikolaievna Borschevaya made her entrance into the world in the icy spring of 1951 while Masha laboured in a wooden dacha in the village of Tanga near Lake Baikal in Siberia.

Ludmilla came next. She was born in a village called Verlch-Surdia in the north of Perm region in 1954.

'It doesn't exist any more,' said Natalya. 'So many of them are deserted now.'

Finally came Anatoly – Dima's Uncle Tolya. He was born in 1959 in a village called Percha, also in the Perm region, and the three children grew up in a little wooden house with no bathroom and an outside toilet.

Natalya talked quickly, recalling the names of great-uncles and aunts, second cousins scattered across Russia. Galina, Anna, Danila, Alexei, Tatiana, Olga.

'Galina was a very talented violinist,' she said.

I wrote it all down. I wanted to remember everything she told me.

*

When she had finished preparing the cucumbers and rinsed the salt from her red, raw hands, she brought the names to life with a box of old sepia photographs – moments in time, snapshots of faraway lives. I looked at their faces and wondered what secrets they could tell me. I stared at them and thought how strange it was that their blood ran in Anya's veins.

I saw Natalya as a five-year-old, dressed up in her best clothes, a white dress and black button shoes, her soft brown curls pinned on top of her head with a neat bow.

I imagined her climbing off the low three-legged stool after the flash had gone off, changing out of her best clothes and stepping outside to play with Luda. After that brief pause in front of the camera, time surged on. She got older, she became a woman, a wife and a mother, and continued on the unstoppable, random journey which carried her, which had carried all of us, from different directions to this point.

Dima returned. I saw him frowning as he looked through my notes, unable to decipher the messy English and shorthand.

He saw me looking at him and smiled, picked up my pen, and at the bottom of my notes about his family tree wrote: 'Maybe enaf?'

That night we went out alone together. Olga stayed with Anya. Dima took a couple of bottles of beer from the fridge and we walked through the dark, unlit streets to the Church of the Saviour. There was a garden behind it. We sat on a stone bench among the dying flowers.

Dima talked about coming to live in England and I didn't

know what to tell him. I felt so tired inside I couldn't speak. I had no words for him. I wasn't thinking about love, I was thinking about survival. I wanted someone to look after me. I didn't want to look after someone else.

'If I stay in the army for another two years I will be able to draw my pension,' he said. 'After that, I will come.'

Two years seemed a long way off. I let him talk and I said nothing.

A bitter, piercing wind swept up from the Usolka river below and he took his coat off, wrapped it around me and pulled me on to his knee. I remembered in a rush how I had first felt about him. He still made me feel safe. But I couldn't imagine him living in England. And I wondered what that meant. For now, the struggle had gone. He had stopped worrying about how difficult it would be for him to come and live with us and I no longer tried to soothe his fears.

We walked home along the moonlit road – our hands clasped together – a world apart.

23

Natalya dressed Anya for the journey home. She tucked her arms and legs into her winter suit and tied the strings of the red hat she had bought under her chin. While Olga, Dima and I carried our bags down the stairs, she sat rocking her on her lap, whispering to her.

When all of our luggage was in the car, we went back upstairs and sat down with Natalya for a minute. It was a Russian tradition, explained Olga. Before setting off on a journey, you pause for a moment and sit.

'It brings good luck to travellers,' she said.

Finally Natalya carried Anya down the stairs. She passed her to Dima who kissed her soft cheeks. Then Natalya did the same. She placed her into the car next to me and pressed a pink carnation into her hand, gently folding her little fingers around the stem.

The driver turned the ignition key and the engine sprang to life. Natalya put her outstretched hand against the window beside her. Anya lifted her head towards her and laughed. The car pulled away. I turned to wave and saw Natalya raising her hands to cover her crumpled face.

At the crossroads in Revolution Square, the car paused at the traffic lights. I looked over at the hotel and wondered if I would ever see it again.

We arrived at Perm just fifteen minutes before the train was due to leave. There was nowhere to park.

Olga ran on ahead while I placed Anya, protesting and kicking, into her buggy and Dima and the driver dragged our bags from the car.

'The train's been delayed,' said Olga in relief, when we caught up with her.

A few minutes later, we boarded the train. Dima lifted Anya's buggy into the carriage.

Olga picked her up decisively.

'I'm taking her for a walk.' she said with a wink and a nod towards Dima and trotted off along the corridor with the driver.

Dima stepped into the compartment and sat down on the seat opposite me, pulling my hands towards his lap and covering them with his own.

He sighed and then said: 'All is good.' I wasn't sure if it was a question or a statement.

I wasn't sure what I felt. The thought of leaving him left a pain in my throat, but I knew I didn't want to take him with me.

He leant forward to kiss me but before our lips met, the train suddenly lurched along the track.

Despite the official half-hour delay, it had begun its journey with no warning.

Dima shouted: 'Goodbye!' and before I had time to reply he planted a hurried kiss on my mouth. He ran down the corridor and disappeared around the corner, yelling at the *provodnitsa* to open the door for him.

At first I thought he hadn't made it to the exit in time. And I was pleased. I thought that he would be carried to Moscow with Anya and I and somehow, on the journey, our differences would melt away.

But I saw him stumble on to the platform. Through the murky window, I saw him for a brief moment, trying to regain his balance after his dramatic exit.

The Kama train caught speed and left him far behind.

Olga returned along the corridor, laughing, with Anya in her arms.

'Well, we nearly took him with us,' she said.

'He didn't have time to say goodbye to Anya,' I said.

Inside my heart was pounding. My mouth was full of the words I had wanted to say. The inadequacy screwed up tightly inside me until my throat felt cramped.

I held Anya close against me and kissed her untroubled face. She was untouched by the unfolding drama of her life.

Olga was reading my thoughts: 'Forget him, Barbara,' she said. 'My grandmother was right. You have your baby, now forget him.'

The journey back to Moscow stretched on and on interminably. The train felt claustrophobic, as if it were holding us in an uncomfortable horizontal limbo between Dima's world and mine.

The air-conditioning had broken down and hundreds of miles before we reached Moscow, smoke, from forest fires which had buried the capital in a choking smog, seeped into the carriage and stung our eyes.

We crossed the Volga river, past Kirov and Nizhny Novgorod, and each mile we gained, I became more impatient to get home.

By the time we reached Moscow, the pain in my throat had gone. Dima and Solikamsk were behind me. My mind raced onwards to home.

As we left our compartment, I turned to check that we hadn't left anything behind. The red banquette seats where Dima and I had sat holding hands were empty. There was nothing to show any of us had ever been there, nothing – except Anya's tiny sticky hand-prints smudged across the wood veneer panelling.

* * *

When I switched my phone on at Heathrow, it started ringing immediately.

It was a message from my editor. He wanted me to go to New York. Tomorrow. It was the anniversary of the attacks on the World Trade Center. He wanted me to soak up the atmosphere and write.

I braced myself as I listened to the message in the middle of the terminal building. My skin prickled. I looked at Anya sitting in her buggy. Her face was smeared with dirt. Her hair was matted and dry. She looked up at me with her big blue eyes and she smiled.

*

That night, while Anya slept I washed my clothes. I waited up for the washing machine to finish its cycle and hung knickers and bras and tops over the radiators. I unpacked and repacked my case and left space for the drying clothes.

In the morning, I took Anya to the childminder's house and kissed her and kissed her until she put her hands up to shield her face and pushed mine away. Then I left her.

I drove back to Heathrow. I flew to New York. I went to Ground Zero and found families of British victims to interview. I stood and listened to Mayor Giuliani read out the names of the 2801 dead and I went back to my hotel room.

I ordered room service and asked them to send up a packet of cigarettes and a box of matches. The windows wouldn't open because of the air-conditioning. I chain-smoked Marlboro Lights and wrote my piece. My head was spinning but it wasn't just the nicotine. I wondered what Dima would have said if I had called him and told him I was in New York. I doubted he would have believed me.

I emailed the article to my editor in London and went out to escape my hazy, smoke-filled room. My flight home wasn't until the following morning. I had never been to New York before and I had an afternoon left to see it. I wondered what I should do. I took a taxi to Barney's and bought a pink velvet jacket for Anya. I crossed the road towards the Empire State Building, bought a ticket and got into one of the elevators. The sky was cloudless and blue. On the 86th floor, the wind was blowing so hard it was difficult to breathe. It blew my hair across my face. I held it back with one hand and stared across the city, past the grey, black and beige skyscrapers to the harbour beyond. The man standing next to me was telling his son that you could see five counties on a day like this. I couldn't take in any of it. My head was filled with Anya.

The distance between us frightened me. She was the most precious thing in the world. I wanted to go home.

24

While I was flying to New York, Dima was fighting again.

I didn't find out until two weeks later. I called him and Natalya answered.

'Dima, nyet! Hospital!' she said, using exactly the same words as before.

His nose was broken. His cheekbone was fractured. One of his eyes was black and swollen.

Late at night while he was walking home, a group of men had stopped him and asked him for a cigarette. He offered them one and they snatched the entire packet. Anyone with half a brain would have cut their losses and walked away. Not in Russia. Not Dima. It was too much of a challenge to his pride. Despite being outnumbered he rose to the bait and the fighting began.

In London, it was a bright, crisp, sunny day. After I'd put the phone down, I took Anya to the swings in the park next to the Houses of Parliament. I pushed her backwards and forwards until she gasped with breathless excitement.

I decided we were alone and we'd manage alone. We didn't need anyone else.

* * *

It was as if we had never been away from our daily whirlwind of messy breakfasts and hurried goodbyes.

Each morning, I dropped Anya off at the childminder's before getting in the car and setting off for Canary Wharf. It was the same old route: around Parliament Square, past the Cenotaph and Downing Street, along Horse Guards Parade. But I saw it with new eyes: a mother's eyes.

Other people's lives no longer seemed so remarkable, but I carried on interviewing and writing: two teenagers who had survived the Bali bombings; a woman with severe post-natal depression who drowned her own baby in the bath; Ann Widdecombe talking about her dramatic weight loss and decision to dye her hair blonde; magician David Blaine reading my mind over the telephone from New York while chewing on pomegranate seeds and apologising for the noise his mouth was making.

'You're thinking of the eight of diamonds, aren't you?' he said in a bored drawl, at the end of a very lengthy card trick.

Sometimes I still thought of escaping. But for now, I didn't think of Dima. I thought of Anya and I living in a cottage somewhere near the sea. I imagined us breathing the clean, salty air and looking for shells on the beach. I pictured us going for midnight moonlit walks together. We would pretend to be explorers on an adventure until Anya was so tired she would fall asleep while I carried her home on my back.

But mostly, I didn't have time to think. I got through one day at a time and the thought of Anya waiting for me at the end of the day kept me going.

And when I collected her in the evening after work and carried her home, I would rub my face against hers and whisper to her: 'It won't be like this for ever.'

But the months were skipping past so quickly.

In November, Anya turned one. I organised a birthday party in a rented hall.

The night before I made a cake. I'd bought a teddybear-shaped tin from the Jane Asher cake shop behind the King's Road in Chelsea. The first cake I made broke in half when I turned it out of the tin. I made another one. I tried to make pink butter icing in the food processor my mother had given me. But it didn't look like butter icing. It looked like plasticine.

At midnight, I cried with frustration. Then I flattened the rubbery pink mess with a rolling pin and prodded it over the cake surface with my fingers. I struck it down with a layer of jam. From a distance – if you squinted – it didn't look too bad.

Everybody came to the party: my father and stepmother; my mother and stepfather; my brother; Anya's godparents and her little friends from the playgroup she attended with her childminder.

I pushed a candle into the teddybear's fat, pink, rubbery stomach and lit it.

We sang 'happy birthday' and Anya took her first steps across the room towards us before falling on to her bottom.

Dima called later that evening. He wanted to offer Anya his 'congratulations'. He said he wanted to come to England and see us but only when his face had healed. It didn't sound great.

'My nose is very bad,' he said.

A doctor had told him it would cost a thousand dollars to fix it.

I wondered how he would ever get the money.

I told him it must have been the most expensive packet of cigarettes he had ever smoked. Then I laughed sarcastically.

He said: 'Not quickly please, Barbara. I am not English man.'

I didn't bother to explain.

* * *

In January, I saw Mr B for the first time in nearly two years. I was in a cafe, drinking cappuccino and writing up an article on my laptop. I looked up and saw him sitting at another table with two other men. I felt strangely calm. I could tell he had already seen me. His cheeks were slightly flushed. I knew that look on his face so well. He was trying to think what to do.

A few minutes later, I looked up again. The table where he had been sitting was empty. Three empty mugs were being cleared away by a waitress. I prickled with outrage. He was a coward. He was too afraid to speak to me. I was angry with myself for caring.

I carried on writing. Suddenly, he was standing at my side. I looked up at him.

He said: 'Hello. How are you?'

I told him I was fine, thank you very much.

He glanced down at my shoes. They were red and velvet and high-heeled.

'I see your taste in footwear hasn't improved,' he said teasingly. He smiled flirtatiously.

He looked at me as if nothing had changed.

I wanted to say to him: 'Have you forgotten? I'm a mother now.'

He hadn't forgotten. He just didn't know what to say to me.

So he said: 'Take care of yourself.'

Then he walked out of the cafe.

I watched him go and I thought: 'My life is nothing to you.'

I wondered how love could be so fickle.

Mr B used to tell me: 'I want to look after you.'

I should have known that he could never do that.

One weekend, we had driven down from London to south Devon, to the Marine Hotel in Salcombe. It overlooked the estuary and we ate Devonshire cream teas and listened to the putt-putting sound of the fishing boats chugging up and down the river. The beach in autumn was deserted. We drew pictures of each other in the sand with driftwood and searched for crabs in rock pools. The cold wind left our cheeks red and smooth. We drank hot chocolate and played Scrabble in a cafe overlooking the sea, and I looked at him with a pain in my heart because I knew he would never be mine.

I knew I should give him up.

When our mugs were empty, we drove back to London and he stopped outside the flat in Balham where I had rented a room. I could tell he was already anxious to get home. He was distracted. His mind was elsewhere. He kissed me goodbye and I climbed out of the car. He drove off before I even reached the front door with my key. When I got inside my room, I lay on my bed and cried into the dazzling pillows.

Now, I was alone again. I couldn't work out how it had happened. My head was muddled. Every moment from the past spun round and round. I couldn't separate them out or make sense of them. I started thinking about old relationships. I started wondering what former loves were doing and how I would feel if I saw any of them again.

So many heartfelt, intimate moments were now nothing more than memories. They had faded away until they no longer meant anything. I thought about the men who had kissed my lips and looked me in the eye and told me they loved me. I had stared right back and said the same. One minute, you belonged to a person and couldn't see beyond them. The next, they meant nothing to you.

I thought about Simon who used to leave flowers stuck to my door at college. He left so many poems and love letters in my pigeon-hole that there could be no doubt in my mind that he loved me. His rooms at Jesus College were just a few steps away from the history library at the Radcliffe Camera. Once, I was in the basement. I couldn't concentrate on Thomas Aquinas' *Summa Theologiae*. I didn't want to dwell with the dead. I kept thinking of Simon in his college rooms a few metres away, alive and strong and vital.

I climbed out of the dark basement into the daylight and

went looking for him. I climbed his staircase and knocked on the ancient heavy wooden door. I heard his voice calling: 'Come in.'

When I walked into the room his face lit up. He closed the copy of Goethe's *The Sorrows of Young Werther* which he had been reading on the desk in front of him. I moved towards him and he pulled me on to his knee and kissed me.

He told me: 'Sometimes I fantasise that you will walk in here one day and tell me you're pregnant.'

I was eighteen. At that age, I didn't know how to be loved like that. It frightened me. I ran away from it. I was cruel to him.

But now when I thought about Simon, I remembered the look on his face when I told him it was over. I remembered watching him cry and how I couldn't bear to witness his pain, knowing that I had caused it.

Now I thought: 'I was loved once. Really loved. And I didn't realise until it was too late.'

I started thinking that perhaps love and truth had little to do with each other. It wasn't that we lie when we are in love. It was that the language of lovers is ephemeral.

When Richard and I had been together for a month, he had sent me a card. On the front, it had a cartoon cat sitting in a tree. The cat had a red nose. He said it reminded him of me when I drank too much wine.

He wrote down how he felt about me. In the card he had written: 'I know I've only known you for a few weeks, but I think I'm in love with you.'

Passion made him reckless. He continued: 'Whatever happens to us in the future, wherever we end up, I want you to know that I will always be here for you.' He underlined whatever, wherever and always. Even as a seventeen-year-old, I thought the implications of that were extraordinary. And I laughed to myself because I knew it couldn't be true. Nobody could be held to such a promise. But he had written it down. It was as binding as a contract.

I had thought: 'One day, when we are worlds apart, I will read this. And commonsense and sanity will stop me coming to find you.'

He was married now. To a nurse. He had two young daughters.

I wondered what he would do if I turned up on his doorstep with the card in my hand and said: 'I need you now and you promised!'

Dima's promise to come and see us appeared emptier than ever.

Sometimes when we spoke on the phone, he would say: 'If my chief will give me holiday I will come in the summer.'

Another time it would be a different story.

'My nose is very bad, Barbara. I don't want you to see my face like this. I will have the operation and come after that.'

I wondered how bad it could really be. I was no longer sure if I wanted to see him. I was too tired to persuade him to make the journey. I wanted him to come of his own volition or not come at all.

It was getting warmer. The courtyard beneath my kitchen window was carpeted with fallen blossom.

*

Dima eventually found the money to have the operation on his crooked nose. He travelled to a hospital in Perm and found a surgeon who didn't charge quite as much as the others. Unfortunately, when the surgeon had finished, his nose looked even worse than before.

Natalya telephoned Olga.

'It looks terrible,' she said. 'He went to a cowboy surgeon. He's so depressed, he's drinking vodka all the time now,' she told her. 'I won't have him in the house. For God's sake, tell Barbara to take him to England. He'll die if he stays here.'

Olga told me that he'd moved out and was renting a room in a flat on the other side of Solikamsk.

I listened and felt nothing. Anya was the only thing that mattered any more.

25

When Anya was eighteen months old I heard from Mr B.

It began innocently enough.

He sent an email asking how I was and I foolishly responded.

He asked me if I had any news.

I sent him a sarcastic reply: 'I've had a baby. I don't know if you've heard.'

He sent another: 'Yes. A beautiful baby girl, I've heard. Is she feisty like her mother?'

He asked if he could see us both.

We met in a cafe near my flat. When I arrived with Anya, he was already sitting in one of the big velvet armchairs near the door. He stood up when we walked in and crouched down beside her. She liked him straight away. She looked up at his big smiling face and let him hold her hand. They went to choose drinks together and she came back with a strawberry milkshake and a straw.

He told me she was wonderful.

'She looks just like you,' he said. 'It's so lovely to see you together. Thank you for agreeing to come.'

Afterwards, we stood on the pavement outside the cafe and said goodbye. He leant forward and kissed me on the cheek.

'We should do this again,' he said. He added: 'If you like.'

I didn't say anything. But I was nodding my head.

A few hours later, he sent me an email. I saw his name in my inbox and I smiled, knowing that I shouldn't. I opened it up and it said: *It was lovely to see you today.*

I smiled a little bit more and moved my eyes down the screen.

Then he said: *There's something you should know. I'm no longer with my wife but I have a ladyfriend I've had for a few months. It's all a bit dull really* . . .

The room started spinning. I heard myself wailing. I raged and I raged.

In my chest, my heart hardened. I wanted it to be made of stone.

* * *

It was getting harder to remember how Russia had made me feel. I no longer thought of salvation. I thought of the past. I thought of history. I thought of another world. But I couldn't see a place for me within it.

One afternoon, when Anya was at the childminder's house and I was working at home, I heard Russian voices.

I was sitting in the kitchen writing up an article on my laptop and their words came floating up through the open window of my third-floor flat.

Two men were standing outside. They were smoking cigarettes. The smell of tobacco smoke mingled with their words. I closed my eyes and remembered.

Later, I met the voices' owners. Sergiy and Vladimir weren't Russian. They were Ukrainian. They were renovating a flat on the ground floor. I took them a cup of sweet, black tea each and they looked at me suspiciously at first.

We talked. Sergiy told me how he learned the Greek alphabet in the back of a lorry on the way to England. He used to run a shoe stall in a town in the west of Ukraine, he explained, but got into problems with 'some mafia guys'.

Vladimir was a ruddy-faced carpenter from Kiev who dreamed of travelling around the world.

'I make the best,' he said, showing the cupboards he had fitted in the kitchen of the flat.

I showed them photographs of Anya and Dima.

'Why isn't he here with you?' asked Vladimir. 'Is he crazy?'

I looked at their strong, stoical, lived-in faces. I was missing Russia. I missed the way it made me feel.

A month later, I was sent back there.

My editor wanted me to write about oil billionaire Roman Abramovich. Olga met me in Moscow and we flew to Ukhta in the Komi Republic in northern Russia where Abramovich had spent his childhood.

It was September and deliciously cold. We found the apartment where he had been raised in Ulitsa Oktyabrskaya. It looked just like Dima's block in Solikamsk: old grey brickwork, cracked tiles and rust-coloured stains from leaking pipes. Weeds and grasses crowded the footpath leading to the front entrance. A young boy on a rickety bicycle circled around the block, staring at us curiously. We climbed the stairs and knocked on a door and a teenage girl agreed to let us in. She showed us into the sitting room of Abramovich's old home. Even the beige wallpaper was the same as Dima's.

We found a bar that sold pizza and gin served with warm flat tonic water and without ice or lemon.

Outside our freezing white breath hovered in the cold night air. Winter was on its way. It made me long for Dima. I called him from the hotel.

I told him: 'I'm in Russia.' At first he wouldn't believe me.

Then he said: 'OK. Please fly to me.'

I told him it was impossible. I was flying back to Moscow the next day and then in the evening, home to London and to Anya. He told me he would take a train to Moscow and come and meet me.

'Please wait for me,' he said. The phone clicked in the receiver.

When I walked into the transit hotel at Sheremetyevo-2 airport the following morning, he was sitting in the foyer with a bunch of red roses on his lap.

He jumped up and walked towards me looking strangely romantic amid the Communist-era furniture. His arms around me felt warm and hard and safe. Despite all the drama, his nose looked almost exactly the same as before. It had a small bump at the bridge, but his face was still beautiful.

He came with me in a taxi to Domodevo airport on the other side of Moscow and the bemused driver watched us kissing in the rear-view mirror.

I liked the feel of his arms around me and his lips on mine. There were butterflies in my stomach. I felt light-headed.

At the airport, he stood in the queue until he could go no further. He kissed me and told me he would come to England. In two months' time. I watched his face as he promised. This time, I saw the way he looked at me. I believed he would come. I wanted him to come.

26

He was easy to spot at the back of the crowd of people sweeping through the arrivals gate at Heathrow Airport. He towered above the other passengers. Even so, he shifted nervously from foot to foot. He was on tiptoe. His eyes were darting around looking for me, as if he was worried that I wouldn't be there. He looked vulnerable and then relieved when he finally saw me waiting, standing by the barrier with Anya asleep in her buggy. He raised his arm in greeting and strode towards us.

He wanted a cigarette. We sat on the edge of the smoking area and he took one out of his coat pocket and lit it. He was carrying a new black sports bag and wearing new clothes: a shiny new navy blue padded jacket which rustled when he lifted his hand to his mouth to smoke; black trousers with a sharp pleat down the fronts of the legs and new black shoes. They were square-toed: the kind that had been fashionable in London five years earlier. He reached inside his jacket and pulled out a Japanese mobile telephone. It looked strange to see something so modern in his hands. The last time I had been to Solikamsk, mobiles were nowhere to be seen. He switched it on and looked at the blank screen. He pressed a few buttons and frowned. 'Not good in England I think,' he said. He switched it off and put it away again.

He carried on smoking. I looked at him closely and tried to take in this new, modern, westernised Dima. He looked at me when he inhaled on the cigarette and I smiled at him. I could smell his skin. It made me feel warm inside. I rested my head on his arm. He took a last drag and stubbed out the cigarette and we walked through the terminal building to the car park. He looked across from the front passenger seat and laughed at the sight of me behind the steering wheel.

'I not believe it!' he said.

I grinned like a maniac. I told him to put on his seatbelt and turned the key in the ignition. The engine sprung to life. We set off for home.

I carried Anya upstairs and placed her in her cot in the bedroom without waking her. Dima and I slept on the sofa bed in the sitting room so we could be alone. We undressed. When his hands touched me, my skin felt as if it was burning beneath his fingers. I wasn't sure if it was him or my lust reawakening. It was two months since I had kissed him in the back of the taxi driving across Moscow. He smelt good and I wanted him.

In the morning, Anya looked at him with jealous eyes.

'My mummy,' she said to him menacingly, holding on to me tightly. He laughed and picked her up.

'This is your daddy,' I explained to her. I pointed at him. 'Anya's daddy.'

She looked at him with curiosity and stopped wriggling in his arms.

He had brought presents: Russian fairytales and Cyrillic alphabet books, lacquered wooden boxes carved by the prisoners at Bely Lebed. Natalya had sent a tiny dove carved out of balsa wood and a set of *matrioshka* dolls.

We took Anya to the playground opposite our block of flats and played football with her. It was November. Dead leaves from the plane trees swirled lightly at our feet and gathered in piles that shimmered and crackled when Anya jumped on them. I looked at the two of them, together. I didn't think about whether I loved him or not. I didn't want to think about it. For now, seeing him with Anya made me happy.

In the afternoon, we went on the London Eye. It seemed a good place to start. Dima carried Anya into our capsule and we took off into the cloudy sky, curving high above the Thames. Rain lashed against the sides. Anya and Dima pressed their noses against the glass and stared at the grey world outside. They wore the same expressions. From the side her face looked like a smaller version of his. It seemed miraculous.

High in the air, London's sprawling mass overwhelmed him. Even in cloud, it stretched on further than seemed possible. The daylight was fading and scatterings of light appeared across the city as night fell.

It was dark when we stepped out of the capsule on to the street below. We walked back home along Albert Embankment towards Lambeth Bridge. We passed groups of teenagers, lovers holding hands and sitting on the wrought-iron benches with views across the Thames to the Houses of Parliament, couples leading tired children home. I wondered if the three of us looked like a family.

Anya wanted me to carry her but the weight of her was making my arms ache. She wouldn't let Dima take her at first. Eventually, forced to choose between him or being returned to her buggy, she opted to ride on his shoulders. He held on to her legs and she clasped her arms around his neck, but she was uncertain. Every now and then she stretched her arm towards me and said: 'Mummy,' – as if to reassure herself that I was still there. I reached up and squeezed her mittened fingers in reply.

The orange lights from the carved street lamps were reflected on the choppy surface of the river.

I took off my gloves and touched the cold night air. It made me think of home and the warmth of a shared bed. I wanted to believe it was real.

27

At the large Sainsbury's supermarket near Vauxhall Bridge, Dima was hovering wide-eyed by the fish counter.

'Where is salt fish please?' he asked. I looked at him apologetically.

So far, the trolley contained two large boxes of Stella Artois. He didn't want vodka. Vodka was for drinking with men, not with the mother of your child.

'I not want drinking this very bad drink with you, Barbara,' he said.

From the chiller cabinet I selected a pot of taramasalata, pickled Orkney herrings, smoked salmon, trout and mackerel. He nodded enthusiastically as I showed each one to him.

He wanted to try English food. I told him that French and Italian and Spanish food was popular in England. He didn't look sure. I had given him a black olive the night before and he had spat it out.

He had tried one once before while on holiday by the Black Sea.

'I remember this berry!' he said, his face contorted in disgust. He washed the taste away with beer.

That night I roasted a chicken. While I cooked, Dima examined my bookshelves. He came into the kitchen with a copy of Laurens Van der Post's *Journey into Russia* in one hand. In the other, he was clasping Anne Applebaum's *Gulag: A History of the Soviet Camps*.

'Very many interesting books,' he said suspiciously with a raised eyebrow. 'Very many interesting Russian books.'

'What do you want to do while you are here?' I asked him later as I cleared the empty plates from the table. 'Where do you want to go?'

He thought for a moment.

'Barbara,' he said, placing his arms around my waist. 'I want look at your big, wonderful city.'

* * *

At 221B Baker Street, Dima was wearing a tweed deerstalker hat and pretending to smoke from the clay pipe in his hand. The Sherlock Holmes museum was a Victorian house styled to look as if it had belonged to the famous detective himself. In the parlour, every tiny detail of Conan Doyle's books had been brought to life. Holmes' violin was there. Letters postmarked from the 1890s lay on a silver platter by the door. Newspapers from the same period were folded up on a table beside the fire. Sherlock Holmes, Dima told me, was rather popular in Russia.

He thrust his camera towards me and posed for a photograph in an armchair next to the fire burning in the grate.

He laughed and laughed at the thought of how much Boris and his friends would laugh when they saw it.

Over the next few days, his camera came out again and again: Dima at the Tower of London with the Yeoman Warders and on Tower Green where Anne Boleyn's head had been chopped off in 1536; Dima next to Henry VIII's over-sized suit of armour; Dima pretending to steal the Imperial State Crown; Dima on Tower Bridge; Dima by Big Ben; Dima in Trafalgar Square; Dima standing on the edge of the Thames pointing towards the MI6 building across the river.

He was starting to look rather dazed. He couldn't believe how many people there were walking along the streets or travelling on the escalators in the Underground. Or how hard it was to walk in a straight line without stopping or being forced to step to the side by the chaotic mass of people.

In Solikamsk, he walked – as everyone did – with his head down, avoiding the bitter, painful wind and keeping his eyes on his feet as he trod precariously across the icy pavements. Dima quickly learnt to walk the London way. Head up, ready to anticipate the random, unguessable moves of those coming towards him. His six-foot-two-inches frame looked taller than ever.

He was entranced by the variety of faces he saw – black, Asian, Chinese – and the different languages he heard being spoken. A Russian couple walked past us and he jumped with excitement and tapped me on the shoulder to point them out: 'Russian peoples!'

As if he had thought he was the only Russian in London.

He tried speaking English.

'Good afternoon,' he said stiffly to a black cab driver when we climbed into the back of a taxi on the way back from one of our trips. The driver frowned at him in his rear-view mirror and ignored him.

Dima looked at me with a puzzled expression on his face.

'I say it wrong?' he whispered.

'It's fine,' I told him. 'I think maybe he didn't hear you.'

At home, Dima went straight into the bedroom and changed his clothes. He had brought just two outfits with him and a pattern had begun to emerge in the days since his arrival. The shiny puffer jacket, pleated trousers, grey-patterned jumper and square-toed shoes were strictly outdoor wear only. Once through the front door, he would fold his trousers and belt neatly over a hanger and put on a pair of shiny blue tracksuit bottoms, a grey t-shirt and plastic flip-flops. Then he would walk into the sitting room and lie down on the sofa.

Today, minutes after lying down, he asked if he could phone his friend in Germany. When their conversation was over, he was excited.

He said: 'Maybe you, Anya and I to make short excursion to Germany to see my friend? To be guests in his house.'

I asked him: 'When?'

'Maybe tomorrow or the day after,' he said. 'We go to Germany by bus.'

I laughed and shook my head and he looked disappointed. He said: 'Why?' He wasn't thinking about the cost or the fact that he didn't have a visa to travel to Germany.

'Ok,' he said, when I pointed out a few of the practicalities. 'No problem. I ask my friend and his wife to come here to London to be guests in your house.'

I smiled weakly, trusting that his friends would find the visa situation just as tricky and that Dima would forget about it.

My one-bedroom flat already felt smaller than ever. I kept tripping over his enormous square-toed shoes in the hall.

I changed the subject. 'We're going to collect Anya now,' I told him. 'You come too.'

I had promised my childminder that I'd bring him to meet her.

Dima sighed and went back into the bedroom to change his clothes again.

Before the day was over, Dima had changed his clothes twice more. After collecting Anya, he hung up his outdoor outfit and donned the shiny tracksuit bottoms and t-shirt once more. He sat at the kitchen table and watched Anya roll out her Play-Doh. He helped her cut out cartoon character shapes from it with plastic cutters.

Later, when she was sleeping, he crept into the bedroom to find his smart trousers and patterned jumper. The babysitter had arrived. We were going out for dinner. He emerged from behind the bedroom door still doing up his belt. It broke in his hands.

'*Oi blin!*' he cursed in Russian. 'It is new belt!'

I wondered if he had bought it from one of the dark-eyed gypsies from southern Russia on one of the dozens of clothing stalls in the market in Solikamsk.

He pulled out his penknife and began fixing the buckle.

We were meeting some of my friends at a Russian restaurant called Potemkin in Clerkenwell. When I said it – 'Pa-temp-kin' – Dima didn't recognize the name of one of Russia's most famous military heroes.

'You know! Pa-temp-kin! Big important Russian man! You remember! Eisenstein film! Battleship Pa-temp-kin!'

My pronunciation had distorted the name beyond recognition. When we arrived and he saw it in giant letters along the side of the restaurant, he slapped the side of his head in recognition.

'Ah! *Patyomkin!*' he said, rolling his eyes at me.

Dima wanted everyone to drink vodka. There were dozens of different kinds on the menu: Russkaya, Sibirskaya, Stolnaya, Stolovaya, Krepkaya. Clear and potent: even the cheapest were several pounds a shot.

He ordered six glassfuls and we drank them down.

We ate little cabbage pies. They were the same as the kind you could buy for just a few roubles from huts on the edge of the road from Perm to Solikamsk.

The room was filled with wealthy Russians. Men wearing sharp suits that hadn't been bought in Moscow. Brassy-looking women with big hair and big jewellery and red nails.

He was listening to their conversations and I was watching his face. It was flushed with excitement. Confident. It was as if the idea of living in London wasn't so ridiculous after all. He was looking at them and thinking: 'If they can survive here, then perhaps so could I.'

He ordered a second round of vodka shots and I swiftly asked for the bill before he could order a third. When it arrived, he picked it up. When he saw how much it came to, the colour drained from his face.

* * *

Money was the biggest gulf between us. I had it and Dima didn't. He didn't have a penny on him. I told him it didn't matter but every time I stood at the checkout at Sainsbury's or paid for tickets to a museum, he looked away awkwardly.

He had never owned a credit card in his life. He didn't even have a bank account. Most Russians didn't trust them. They wanted to see their money in their hands. In Solikamsk, I never thought about money. Dima didn't seem to have much, but it didn't matter. Bits of food and the odd bottle of beer or vodka didn't cost much. Nor did trips to friends' houses or mushroom picking or visits to the river.

In London, I was spewing out money wherever we went: taxis fares, coffees, café and restaurant bills, money for Anya's childminder.

I produced my gold card like a magic key to a bottomless bank account with an enormous overdraft facility. I looked at myself through his eyes and I didn't like what I saw.

My car was booked in for its annual service. We drove to the Ford garage in Wimbledon.

'What's wrong with car?' he asked, looking at me as if I was stupid. 'Car is going. No problem. Why you go to garage?'

I gave a brief, simplified explanation of the benefits of annual servicing and paintwork warranties.

'Keep car nice,' I told him, patting the dashboard. He wasn't listening.

'I think you give your money for nothing,' he said impatiently. He moved his hands as if he was screwing up paper and throwing it out of the window.

I handed over my car keys to a woman on the service

reception desk and sat down in the waiting area. Dima walked around the showroom and sat in one of the shiny, flawless cars. He looked like a little boy sitting behind the steering wheel.

A salesman closed in on him: 'How does it feel, sir? Have you noticed how the seat has been designed to emulate the natural contours of the back.'

Dima stared back at him. 'I only want looking,' he growled. The salesman swiftly withdrew.

It was going to be a couple of hours before the car was ready. We set off on foot towards Wimbledon Lawn Tennis Club. Dima wanted to have his picture taken on Centre Court. In Russia, tennis was even more popular than Sherlock Holmes, he said.

His visit was starting to remind me of the time my French exchange partner came from Cherbourg to stay with me at home in Portsmouth when I was thirteen. I spent the week with a sulky, bored face, showing her the city. We went on a tour of HMS *Victory* with my father and stepmother and saw Nelson's old hammock and examined the exact spot on the deck where he fell. We stood at the top of Southsea Castle and stared out across the Solent to the Isle of Wight and the distinctive steeple of All Saints Church in Ryde. We went to the D-Day Museum on the edge of Southsea Common.

I wasn't sharing my life with Dima, I was showing it to him. And none of it meant anything to me. It wasn't real. The only time I'd ever been to Wimbledon was to write about the scandalous price of strawberries and cream.

The lady from the service reception desk called on my mobile phone. My car needed three new tyres, she said. It wasn't going to be cheap. I sighed and agreed. Dima asked what was happening and I told him.

'You are crazy,' he said, tapping the side of his head. 'I think these people are big gangsters.'

I thought about how little Dima knew about me. He wasn't even scratching at the surface. I was tired of being a tourist. My mind was elsewhere. It was forever churning practicalities over and over: should I be bringing up a child in central London, or should I move out of the city. How long I would be able to manage working and looking after Anya. How long could we stay in a one-bedroom flat. My head was filled with mortgages and bank accounts and work.

I was worrying, and I couldn't share any of it with Dima.

I wanted someone to look after me.

On the way back to the garage, he reached for my hand. It felt cramped and hot in his. I wanted to wriggle my fingers and yank it free.

He let go so he could light a cigarette. I asked him if I could have one and he said: 'No. It's very bad.'

It was a bleak November day. It was raining lightly, but too windy for an umbrella. We stood still for a moment so he could strike a match behind his coat. The cold and damp was starting to seep into my shoes.

After he'd finished smoking, he tried to hold my hand again. I pretended not to notice and put it deep into my pocket out of his reach. I didn't want to pretend that we were together when I felt so alone.

*　*　*

My mother was coming for lunch. There was a knock at the door. Dima ran into the bedroom to change his clothes.

'Hello darling,' she said breezily as she stepped into the hall. Anya tugged on her long denim skirt excitedly and ran towards the bedroom door. She pushed it open to reveal Dima, standing there, his trousers halfway up his legs.

'My Daddy!' she announced proudly.

'Hello!' he said, frantically pulling up his trousers with one hand while trying to close the door with the other.

My mother liked him.

'I thought he had a lovely nature, darling,' she said on the telephone a couple of days later. 'He seemed very kind and gentle.'

Dima had given her another one of the delicately carved balsa wood doves in a little box and they sat together with my giant Russian/English dictionary making conversation while I chopped vegetables in the kitchen.

I admired him for not being shy and awkward. He was determined to talk in English.

He said: 'My mother sends greetings to you,' and my mother thanked him and sent them back.

I smiled inwardly at the sound of him. He was on his best behaviour. He wanted to make a good impression.

I was touched that it mattered so much to him.

But it wasn't enough.

28

Dima had been in London for exactly a week. He was staying for a fortnight, but I had to go back to work. I wondered what he would do while I was out. He wouldn't let me give him any money. The bag he had brought from Russia was filled with dozens of gold cartons of his favourite Russian brand *Yava Zolotaya*. He had brought enough to last him for the duration of his visit and he didn't need anything else.

He said he'd go for long walks and look around art galleries.

On Monday morning, I woke up at seven. Dima was still asleep, his face half-hidden beneath the duvet. I lifted Anya out of her cot and she followed me into the kitchen. I drank black coffee and fed her banana porridge. I dressed her and she sat on the bathroom floor watching me while I showered.

I looked at her turning the pages of her pop-up jungle book and I wondered if she understood who Dima was. At the beginning of his visit she had been confused and unsettled, then excited to see a new face. She liked the feeling of being lifted up in strong arms until she could stretch up and touch the ceiling. When he was sleeping she hardly seemed aware of him at all. They were bound up together by blood ties, but relationships weren't so effortless.

She didn't have a care in the world. She was saying the names of the animals out loud and lifting up the book to show me the pictures and I thought how trusting she was, how dependent she was on me for her happiness.

We left the house hand-in-hand. I shouted goodbye to Dima on the way out.

Just before the front door slammed shut, I heard a muffled murmur from the bedroom.

At the childminder's house, I let go of Anya's hand and she stood on the doorstep waving goodbye to me. I looked at her and saw myself as a child.

I was four. It was summer. The tree in our front garden was dense with firm emerald green leaves. I liked pulling them off and running my fingers over the jagged edges and the crisp ridged veins on their undersides. I was standing on the orange terracotta doorstep with my grandparents. My mother was gliding across the lawn. I saw her from her feet up: her dark brown leather-thong sandals, then the white cheesecloth of her long halter-neck sundress. It was rippling around her ankles as she moved.

Her feet were carrying her away from the house towards her car. She was leaving again. I ran after her and held on to her skirt. I felt the soft fabric scrunched up in my fist and saw the narrow beige stripe that ran diagonally through the material.

She stopped and stood still. Arms reached after me, pulling me back and away from her. Hands bigger than mine peeled my fingers from around her feet, one by one by one.

* * *

It was a relief to be back in the office. I felt as if I could breathe again. The *Mirror*'s open-plan newsroom stretched out around me. Space and light. As the day drew on, I thought of Dima sitting in my flat, waiting for me to return. In the afternoon, he called me to ask: 'What time you come back?' His voice sounded alien and intrusive. I knew I wasn't being fair, but I sounded irritated when I replied.

I snapped: 'I don't know.'

He was halfway down the stairs when I pulled up outside my block of flats with Anya in the back of the car.

I had no keys. I'd left mine with Dima in the morning. I lifted Anya up to press the buzzer.

'Hello, my darling,' he said. 'Please come.' I stared at the intercom speaker. His voice sounded unnatural and oppressive. It made me think that we were both playing roles. It wasn't real.

He came halfway down the stairs to meet us.

'I want use your telephone,' he said urgently.

'Of course,' I said, and asked him what was wrong.

'Come, quickly please,' he said.

Inside the flat, there was a strong smell of fish. He pulled me into the sitting room where the television was on loud.

He pointed to the screen.

It was one of those competitions where they ask you a really easy question and ask you to phone in the answer: *a, b or c. Calls cost £1.*

The capital of France is *a Paris or b London or c Moscow.*

Despite his poor English, Dima had worked out the answer and was beside himself with excitement.

'I know! I know! I know!' he said over and over again. 'Please give me telephone.'

I told him it was a con.

'They make the answer as easy as possible so that as many people as possible telephone in,' I explained.

When he looked at me blankly, I added: 'Big gangsters!'

He held his hand out for the phone.

'Dima, no. You'll never win,' I told him.

He walked sulkily out of the sitting room into the kitchen.

I followed him.

'I make you dinner,' he said, lifting the lid off a saucepan. Inside the heads of several rainbow trout floated in a pan of steaming water with chopped herbs.

I let out a cry.

'Oh God,' I said. 'Where did you get those.'

He opened the freezer door. Inside were the decapitated trout bodies which had been ripped from their polystyrene trays. He smiled with a boyish expression on his face – as if he was waiting for me to congratulate him on his resourcefulness.

'I am good kitchen boy!'

'I'm sorry, Dima,' I said. 'I can't eat that.'

His face darkened. His eyes narrowed to thin slits.

'You know nothing about good food,' he said.

* * *

When I was at home, I couldn't find any space to be alone. The flat smelled permanently of cooked fish and man. It was starting to feel as if I couldn't breathe. The walls were pressing in on me.

I knew it wasn't his fault and I felt guilty for wishing he wasn't there.

Every day when I came home from work, Dima would be lying on the sofa watching television.

I'd sit Anya at the kitchen table in her plastic booster seat and let her paint to keep her distracted while I cooked or washed up or filled out expenses sheets for work or sorted through paperwork and bills.

Occasionally, he'd get up, walk to the kitchen and get a can of beer from the fridge.

Sometimes he'd say to me: 'Please, come and sit,' as if I had all the time in the world to sit around drinking beer with him. I kept telling myself that it wasn't his fault but he constantly reminded me how far apart we were.

I'd snap at him irritably: 'I've got too much to do. I'll come in a minute.'

I kept hearing my voice telling him: 'Go and sit down. I'll sort it out.' Maybe I'd been looking after myself for too long. I didn't know how to share my responsibilities with him.

I asked him if he would paint the ceiling in the hallway. I thought it would give him something to do and I thought he would be happy to feel he was helping me out. He said he would do the painting but only if I washed the ceiling first. He said that washing was a woman's job. We argued about it and eventually he gave in, but not before he had tried another tactic to get out of it.

'I have no clothes for painting,' he said.

I smiled and told him: 'Take them off and paint naked. There'll be no one here to see you.'

When I arrived home with Anya the next day, the hall ceiling was brilliant white.

Dima was in the kitchen, washing dishes. I looked at him standing at the sink. My Russian lieutenant was wearing blue Marigolds. They were far too small. The rubber was stretched tightly over the backs of his large hands.

There was half a lemon on the counter. It had been there for days and was wrinkled and dry. The peel was thin and brittle. I picked it up and dropped it into the bin.

Dima pounced.

'No!' he shouted. 'It's good food.' He reached into the bin and pulled it out with one of his blue-gloved hands.

'Put it back,' I insisted.

'Barbara, please look,' he said. He took a fork out of the drawer and stabbed it into the flesh.

'Look!' he said as the juice ran down his hand. He thrust the lemon close to my face. 'It's good food.'

I told him: 'It's my bloody lemon. I paid for it and I'll throw it away if I want to.'

I thrust it to the bottom of the bin, slammed the flip-top and walked out of the kitchen.

I ran a bath for myself. It had become a nightly ritual. The bathroom was the only place I could be alone. I'd wallow in the hot, fragrant water until my fingers and toes were pink and wrinkled, and think resentfully of him lying in my bed, waiting for me. Sometimes I'd lie in there so long he'd have fallen asleep by the time I came out. I'd climb into bed as slowly as I could to avoid waking him. I couldn't sleep. I'd lie awake staring at the ceiling. I could hear Anya's soft breathing coming from the cot in the corner. Next to me, Dima would snore. I couldn't stand it.

I was starting to wonder how much more my nerves could take.

* * *

I'd already been working for a couple of hours when Dima emerged from the bedroom in the morning. I was working at home, writing up an interview.

He came into the kitchen where I was sitting at the table and spread slices of soft white bread with thick layers of bright pink taramasalata. He took a can of beer from the fridge. He carried his breakfast into the sitting room and put on the television. It was loud. I couldn't work. I went in and asked him to turn it down. He lazily stretched out an arm for the remote control, lifted it and pointed it towards the television. I still couldn't concentrate. The banal sound of daytime television drifted into the kitchen and grated on my nerves. After an hour, I couldn't stand it any more.

I walked into the sitting room and told him: 'For God's sake, go out. Just go out.'

I grabbed his coat and handed it to him. I placed a *London A–Z* in his pocket.

'Go out and see big, wonderful city,' I said, pushing him firmly out of the door.

'And don't come back before six.'

*

At 8 p.m. there was still no sign of him.

I'd finished writing up my interview hours earlier. Anya was in bed. I had cooked dinner and opened a bottle of wine. I had already drunk two glassfuls. I was feeling guilty about my treatment of him. I had been too hard on him. I wondered if he was deliberately staying out late to punish me.

At 9 p.m. the intercom buzzer rang.

'It is me, my darling,' he announced.

When he reached my front door, I asked him where he had been all day.

He laughed and said: 'I have had very interesting meeting with your police.'

At first I thought he was joking, but his face became deadly serious.

After I had ejected him from the flat, he had walked all the way from Westminster to Tower Bridge.

On his way home, despite the fact that it was getting dark, he decided to have a quick look at Buckingham Palace. He walked into St James's Park.

Dima wasn't the only person visiting Buckingham Palace that night. US President George Bush was due to arrive around the same time. Armed police were swarming over the area. When they found Dima wandering around the park taking photographs in the dark, they weren't impressed.

A police van roared through the park gates towards him. Ten officers jumped out of the back and stood around him in a circle.

When they asked what he was doing, he answered: 'Not quickly please, I am not English man.'

They asked to see some identification and he slowly put

his hand into his coat to pull out his passport.

'Which hotel are you staying at?' asked one officer.

Dima told them he wasn't staying at a hotel, but he couldn't remember my address either.

In the end he showed them my street on the map I had given him. He waved the front door key at them. One of the police officers inspected his camera, accompanied him out of the park and told him:

'Listen mate. You shouldn't be here. Take my advice and get yourself home.'

* * *

I was starting to dread coming home. As soon as I turned the key in the lock I could hear the television. He would be lying on the sofa in his t-shirt and shiny tracksuit bottoms. He would look bored. There would be a couple of empty beer cans on the window sill next to him. He had spent hours playing games on his mobile phone, the screen just inches from his nose. But a flat battery and no charger meant that even that pleasure had gone now.

He would be waiting for me to come home and the thought of it made me recoil inside. I couldn't bear the idea that someone else needed me so much. I wondered what that said about me. Maybe I was the problem. Maybe I was emotionally crippled somehow, unable to love and be loved. I wondered if that was true. I wasn't even sure that Dima really loved me. Not really.

When I pulled up outside the flat, I remembered all the times I had done so in the past, wondering, hoping that Mr B's car would be there waiting for me.

I didn't do that any more. After the meeting in the cafe with

Anya, I wrote to him. I told him:

I don't want you in my life any more. You bring everything upon yourself, your lying and cheating. Your cowardice. It makes me feel sick. I don't want a part in it any more.

I despise the life of lies you lead. And I despise myself for acquiescing in it.

If we wanted to be together, we'd be together. And we're not. End of story.

End of story.

I pushed the intercom buzzer.

'Hello my darling,' said Dima. When I got upstairs, he was sitting at the kitchen table with my steam iron in front of him in pieces. The hotplate had been unscrewed and several wires were hanging out. In the absence of a phone charger, he had found another way to power up his mobile. A wire from the iron led straight into the bottom of the handset. It was a miracle he hadn't electrocuted himself or set fire to the flat.

'It's no problem. All to be good,' he said, when he saw my face. He stood up from the table.

I put down my bags and kept moving about so he couldn't kiss me. He casually draped his arm around me. I couldn't bear the feel of it across my shoulders. I ducked down and slipped away from him. I walked into the bathroom and locked the door. When I came out, I picked up my keys in the hall and called to him: 'I'm going to collect Anya,' before running out of the front door and back down the stairs again.

After Anya had gone to bed, I locked myself away in the bathroom. Cocooned in the hot water, I felt wild and rebellious.

I wished I had taken one of his cigarettes. I wanted to lie in the bath and smoke.

Dima knocked and asked what I was doing.

I stared resentfully at the white door and I told him: 'I won't be long.'

I took so long he gave up on me. When I came out, he was asleep on the sofa. His long legs were hanging over the edge of the arm. He was snoring softly. I put a blanket on him and closed the sitting room door. I walked into the bedroom. I climbed alone into the big white bed and stretched my arms and legs across the smooth cool cotton.

Sleep carried me back to another time and place:

I am seventeen again. It is summer. I am cycling along Salterns Road with the sea at my side. And Richard is waiting for me. The hedgerows and the yellow-flowering gorse bushes with their musty green smell whizz by either side of me. Warm air is rushing past my ears. I can hear the purring sound my bicycle wheels make when I stop pedalling and coast along the tarmac. The road ahead curves to the right along the beach and then back uphill. The Solent is sparkling and blue. The sails on the yachts are taut and full. I can taste the sea air in my mouth. My heart is beating hard and clear. My blood is rushing around my body. In a few minutes I will be there. Richard is waiting for me.

I turn into his road, my back to the sea. Past the row of pine trees at the top of the front garden, into the driveway. The front door is already wide open. He is waiting.

29

It was Dima's last night in England. I cooked him roast beef and Yorkshire pudding. I smothered it in gravy. I made apple pie and heated ready-made custard in a pan. I opened a bottle of claret. Dima said he had never seen anything so magnificent.

He said: 'You are wonderful woman. I think I to be dreaming of your food when I am in Russia.'

He couldn't finish it. He pushed his plate away, sat back and patted his stomach with a satisfied sigh.

I opened the large sash window so he could smoke. He sat on the kitchen counter next to it and looked out over the floodlit courtyard below. I stood between his legs with my back to him, resting my elbows on his knees. I took a drag on his cigarette and blew the smoke out into the freezing night.

I said to him: 'Tell me why your marriage to Tanya ended.'

Dima sighed. He ground out his cigarette on the window sill and flicked it into the courtyard below. He began talking: slowly, reluctantly at first. Then he found his rhythm. He didn't stop until he had finished.

*

He had a best friend – another soldier with whom he had served in Spetsnaz – Russian Special Forces. Such was the bond between them that they would have died for each other. They both lived in the Siberian city of Krasnoyarsk. They married and had children. His friend had a son. He and Tanya had their daughter, Yulia. Then his friend's wife was diagnosed with cancer. She died. At the funeral, Dima helped his friend carry her coffin. Together, they lowered it into the ground and began scattering spadefuls of earth over the smooth wooden lid.

A few weeks later it was New Year's Eve. Across Russia, families were celebrating with New Year trees and presents. In the afternoon, Dima called in to check on his broken-hearted friend. He found him sitting in the darkness with his young son. Dima said to him: 'You are coming home with me. You will celebrate the New Year with me and with my family.' He took them back to the flat he shared with Tanya.

In the evening, they put the children to bed. Tanya cooked a meal. The three of them ate and began drinking.

Dima went outside to smoke a cigarette. When he returned, he saw his friend and his wife kissing passionately. He said nothing. He went back outside again and came back in, this time making as much noise as he could. They had pulled apart by the time he walked into the kitchen. Still he said nothing. His friend stayed the night on the sofa. Dima slept next to his wife. Only in the morning, when his friend and his son had gone back home, did Dima finally speak.

He could forgive his friend, half-crazed with grief, but not his wife. Despite her tears, he told her he was leaving her. Once he had made up his mind, it was set in stone. Nothing could change it.

He requested a transfer and was offered a position at the prison in Solikamsk. He left Siberia and went back to live with his mother. Thrown together by a moment's madness, Tanya and his best friend eventually married.

I thought: 'If it hadn't been for that brief kiss, that moment of betrayal, Anya would never have been born.'

When his wife saw desire in Dima's friend's eyes and leant forwards to kiss him, she paved the way for Anya's birth. Fate crowded in on me. My head spun with thousands of random moments. Desire, betrayal, love. I wondered if we were meant to be together after all. Everywhere I looked, love seemed so imperfect: transient, fickle, flawed, dishonest. Perhaps Dima and I were no different. We weren't perfect. But perfection would bring its own burdens and pressures anyway. Maybe we were perfectly imperfect. Maybe if we started out from that platform of understanding, there would be no expectations and no disappointments. We had a child together. We would be all right somehow.

But I didn't really believe that. Not me. Not the girl who used to cycle down Salterns Road with the sea air on her face and fire in her heart.

Dima had finished telling his story. His face looked sad and tired. I stroked his hair and kissed his temple. The skin there tasted salty on my lips. I had never felt so much for him, but he didn't look like a saviour any more. I was going to have to save myself.

I cradled his head against my chest. I felt love and sorrow and confusion.

* * *

In the morning, we drove to Heathrow.

Anya wanted to wear her bright red spotted ladybird wellies. I was happy to do anything to distract her. It was only her second car journey since I had taken her out of nappies. She sat in the back of the car in her seat clutching her toy puppy, Pasha, unaware that her father was leaving. Dima kept twisting around from the front to talk to her. The strap of his new bag had broken. His penknife was out again and he was trying to fix it.

In the departure lounge, we said goodbye with kisses and hugs. He picked up Anya and spoke tenderly to her. His voice was steady, but his breathing sounded laboured and shaky. Slowly, he passed her back to me and kissed me once more.

Anya kicked to be put down and I set her on her feet beside me, holding on to her hand.

Dima walked through the zig-zagging cordoned-off walkway with his mended bag over his shoulder. Each time the walkway twisted back on itself towards us, he looked up and smiled.

Anya was tugging on my hand urgently. I looked down and followed her gaze. She was staring at a glossy red Postman Pat van ride. Its lights were flashing. It was playing a song.

'Pat! Pat!' she shouted, trying to pull me towards it.

'In a minute,' I told her. 'Just wait for a minute.'

She started to cry and I bent down to pick her up. I stroked her curls and kissed her soft cheeks.

I turned to wave one final goodbye to Dima, but the walkway was empty. Nothing is for ever.

He had already gone.

Epilogue

You are four years old. You like lollipops and riding your bike and being pushed high on the swings by the Houses of Parliament. You love going to the sandpit in front of our flat and jumping in the paddling pool with just your pants on. You want your tiny toenails to be bright pink like mine but when I paint them you never sit still long enough to let them dry.

You hate having your hair brushed – 'You're pulling my head off!' – and going to bed: 'But I'm not tired, Mummy.'

Sometimes when you wake up in the middle of the night, you climb quietly into my bed and think I won't notice. You like my bed better than yours. You tell me its soft whiteness is cosier. I feel you slip in beside me clutching your teddybear blanket and your toy puppy, Pasha. I feel your warm little body next to me. Your legs are long and strong and your skin is tanned like your father's. You think I don't notice you reach out your hand and hold on to my arm. But I do.

You told me once: 'You are my family and I am your family. And that's just the way life is.'

You are wiser than your years.

You ask so many questions. And I want to answer them all, but I don't always know how.

> *Where does the earth end?*
> *Where does a circle begin?*
> *Why don't aeroplanes go into space?*
> *Why doesn't my Daddy live with us?*

You don't remember the time he came to stay with us. And when I tell you about it – how you were jealous of him at first; how you told him off if he dared, instead of me, to push you in your buggy – you laugh at your former self as if she was another, different girl.

> *Who do I love more: you or my Daddy?*

Your father is a hero.

You tell your teachers at school: 'My Daddy is Russian and he shoots bears in the forest.'

And I don't say anything. I smile and I stroke my hand across the top of your head because you are too young to understand how complicated love is. You are too small to know that there are no saviours.

It's too soon to tell you that in the end, you have to save yourself.

I am watching you grow and I'm waiting.

You are like a brightly coloured *matrioshka* doll being put together, each little figure covered by a slightly larger one as the months pass. I marvel at how tall you have grown and how your plump toddler cheeks are smoothing out into the milky skin of a little girl.

If I could peel back all the layers, somewhere I would find the tiniest one of all, the newborn baby, the one who could see no further than me.

But you look beyond me now.

Yours eyes are open to the world. And you long to see the things that are hidden from view.

I will show them to you.

When are we going to see my Daddy in Russia?

One day, I will take you to see him. I think we'll go by train, so you can see how the light changes as we move east. I'll let you sleep on the top bunk so you can lie staring out of the window towards the tops of the trees with leaves in more shades of red and gold and brown than there are names for.

On our way there, I will tell you again about the moment I first saw your father and how I think of him whenever I smell crushed dill or feel vodka burning on my lips.

I will tell you how, when I first held you in my arms, I thought: 'If nothing ever happens to me ever again, it won't matter.'

Anyinky, malinky, horoshinky. Little Anya, little one, little beauty.

I'll take you to see him and I'll show you the lopsided stairs leading up to his apartment by the railway track. I'll take you on to the balcony and we'll stand among the dusty African violets and look out across the Usolka. We'll sit down together – your father, you and me – and we'll eat Natalya's cabbage soup, thick with smetana. We'll toast each other with sweet Georgian wine.

When you are old enough, I will tell you a story about a town far away in the Ural mountains and the beautiful blue-eyed lieutenant who is your father.

I will hold you close in my arms and tell you never to forget that you are my miracle child, conceived in a cockroach-ridden room on turquoise nylon sheets while your mother dreamed of life and love.